MW01047664

Na**TiV**ity
Dramas

Four Nontraditional
Christmas Plays
For All Ages

Keith Hewitt

CSS Publishing Company, Inc., Lima, Ohio

NATIVITY DRAMAS

Copyright © 2007 by
CSS Publishing Company, Inc.
Lima, Ohio

The original purchaser may photocopy material in this publication for use as it was in-
tended (worship material for worship use; educational material for classroom use; dra-
matic material for staging or production). No additional permission is required from the
publisher for such copying by the original purchaser only. Inquiries should be addressed
to: Permissions, CSS Publishing Company, Inc., 517 South Main Street, Lima, Ohio 45804.

For more information about CSS Publishing Company resources, visit our website at
www.csspub.com or email us at csr@csspub.com or call (800) 241-4056.

Cover design by Barbara Spencer and Nikki Nocera
ISBN-13: 978-0-7880-2483-2
ISBN-10: 0-7880-2483-3   PRINTED IN USA

This book is dedicated

to my wife, Rachel,
who has never been bothered by the ambiguity
of being both my chief critic and head cheerleader
for more than two decades;

to my family,
who has always been there to encourage me;

to the Sunday school teachers and students
of Wilmot United Methodist Church, past and present,
who manage each year to take words on paper and transform
them into reality onstage;

and to the people of Wilmot UMC
who over the years have been willing
to forego "normal" Christmas pageants
for something less traditional, but maybe a little more fun.

We've all learned that sometimes the best way
to see something better
is to look at it from a different perspective.

Table Of Contents

Introduction

When I was a child, going to Sunday school instead of teaching it, my church used to put on a Christmas program every year. It was not a Christmas pageant, but simply a telling of the Christmas story in song and narrative, with each grade doing a couple of songs, and reciting (in unison) a passage from scripture telling some part of the story. It was simple, it was direct, and so help me, it was the exact same program every year — year after year, from kindergarten through seventh grade.

One of the unintended consequences of this, by the way, is that there are certain Christmas songs that just don't sound right to me unless they're being yelled, unmelodically, by a group of six- and seven-year-olds. There are also some songs that are not in our hymnal, or even part of my conscious memory, that I could still sing today, all these decades later, if properly cued by the opening bars played on a slightly-off-key piano. The creators of *The Manchurian Candidate* could have learned a thing or two from the lady who directed our Christmas program.

Times change, and people change with them. I found myself, many years later, at another church, actually teaching Sunday school. When the subject of a Christmas program came up, I flashed back to my youth and winced. "How about doing something a little different?" I suggested to the Sunday school superintendent — who also happened to be my wife.

"What do you mean?" she asked suspiciously, as wives are wont to do.

"I mean everybody already knows the Nativity story — the inn, the stable, all that stuff. Certainly everybody who's going to be sitting in our church, watching it, knows the story. So why just tell the same old story that everybody already knows?"

"So what story would *you* tell?" she challenged.

"Basically the same story — but through someone else's eyes. And we can tell it with a little different setting. Something the children will be able to relate to."

And thus was born "Ewe's Clues," a variation on the Nativity story told with a tip of the hat to the popular Nickelodeon television series *Blue's Clues*.

The children had a blast, the parents and grandparents enjoyed the show — and in the course of doing the play, they even managed to convey a deeper message about the coming of the Messiah, and what it meant to one particular shepherd two thousand years ago. And from that play, a series of plays was born.

The plays in this book have all been "field tested" by the Sunday school students of Wilmot United Methodist Church. They were written with the concept of taking a modern television show back 2,000 years and turning it loose just in time to cross paths with the Nativity story. For the most part, the main characters are not what we think of as principals in the Christmas story — instead, they are ordinary, working people who just happen to have stumbled across a turning point in history. Their actions and reactions to that moment in time — and whether or not they even recognize it — are what make the story.

And, of course, it's fun to think of what might have been. Who *hasn't* wondered what *CSI* would have been like 2,000 years ago, or what it would have been like to take a camera along while *COPS* patrolled the mean streets of Bethlehem in 4 BC?

You haven't? Then read on....

General Production Notes

Each of the plays in this book is designed to be produced in a church — specifically, a church without a dedicated stage. The sets are simple, generally meant to be sketched in behind and around the actors, to give the audience a feel for where and when they are, rather than to attempt to transport them to the Bethlehem or Jerusalem of 2,000 years ago. Thus we might have a table and chairs and some tableware for one scene, which are then easily picked up and transported offstage by the actors (or stagehands, if you're lucky enough to have such), to make way for the manger in the next scene.

This requires more coordination than you might imagine, if you haven't ever put on a play, and it's not a bad idea to practice it with your cast for several rehearsals before they actually perform the play, to give them a chance to get used to it. Also, somebody other than the actors should be in charge of keeping the props (including furniture) organized by scene, so that you can be sure the right things are on stage when you need them ... or you may find one of your characters improvising by pulling out a credit card, when he should be handing over a coin purse; or that the camel, central to the scene, is nowhere to be found when the scene starts.

Did I say camel? Yes. Over the years of putting on these plays at our church, probably the most challenging single prop for any of the plays in this collection was the camel from the traffic stop in "COPS: Bethlehem." Most of the other items could be bought or borrowed, but oddly enough, nobody in our congregation had a life-sized camel that we could borrow.

Fortunately, we are blessed with several gifted artists in our congregation, and they were able to create a two-dimensional cardboard camel for us. It stood about three to four feet tall at the hump, and the cardboard was folded over at the bottom to form a base so it would stand. A 2x4 would probably do the job, also. A little paint, a fancy rope around its neck, and *voila* — a ship of the desert. Would anyone watching the play mistake it for a live camel? No. But would anyone watching the play know what it was supposed to be? Yes. And that's all we needed.

9

That's all you need, too. And someone you know can do it for you, too. Every congregation is a mix of many talents, many gifts — if you don't already have someone in mind, just put the word out, and if there isn't someone in your church who can do it, there's someone who knows someone who can. Ask, and it will be given unto you.

If you're just getting started at doing Christmas pageants, you should start looking for costume accessories around Halloween. Such things as helmets, swords, spears, and other accessories are generally easier to find then. It's been our experience that finding a Roman-style costume helmet is just not as easy as you might think at any other time of year.

In the end, it's important to remember that you're putting on a play, not a documentary. After all, when the title of your pageant is "CSI: Bethlehem," the audience already knows that gritty realism isn't going to be the strong suit of your production. The props are there to help move the story along, to give the actors tools to work with and (sometimes) advance the plot — if you can only find a Greek helmet, instead of Roman, it's not really a problem; if your papyrus scroll is pieces of printer paper taped together and rolled up, that will work. Just stay within the loose bonds of reality.

Of course, once you have your props, along with other actual costumes and other items that you might come into possession of (even including the occasional camel), it's not a bad idea to find a place to keep them at the church, if you have room. Most of them are going to get reused from year to year — and even if the script doesn't call for it, you can always improvise. Every script can use a camel, somewhere!

Ewe's Clues:
A Christmas Story

Characters (in order of appearance)
    Narrator (offstage)
    Stephen
    Ewe (a sheep)
    Sheep (indeterminate number)
    Hay Bale 1
    Hay Bale 2
    Donkey
    Magi 3
    Magi 2
    Magi 1
    Old Shepherd

Costumes

Use appropriate costumes for the characters. Try cardboard boxes sprayed with glue and sprinkled with hay for the hay bales — cut out arms and head spaces. The sheep may be very elaborate with full sheep costumes or as simple as a mask made with cotton balls on a paper plate.

Props

    Rock
    Four "hoofprints" with sticky backs
    Scroll
    Quill
    Spotlight

(The scene opens with Stephen, a shepherd, sitting on a rock at center stage. He seems lost in thought, and as the scene opens he pulls his robe tighter about himself, as though cold. There are a couple of sheep grazing nearby.)

Narrator: I was young once, you know. Hard to believe, isn't it? But I was — I was young once. And I was a shepherd. The most boring job I ever had, it was. I mean, being outdoors and all is nice, but it loses its charm the first night it drops below freezing. And the sheep — they aren't the brightest animals God ever put on the earth —

(Sheep stop grazing long enough to look up, as though searching for the voice.)

Narrator: You get mighty bored and mighty lonely out there when the night is long and the wind is cold. You start to do things to entertain yourself, keep yourself sharp so the wolves don't steal the flock out from under you. Lucky for me there was one smart sheep in the flock I watched — a sheep that liked to play games. Yep, she was a mighty special sheep, that one. I still think about her every now and then — and I think about the night that changed everything —

(Ewe comes up beside Stephen and nuzzles him. Absentmindedly, the shepherd reaches down and scratches her head.)

Stephen: Hi, Ewe. Getting enough to eat?

(Ewe bleats and nods her head.)

Stephen: Good. I wish I could say the same.

(Ewe bleats sympathetically, rubs up against Stephen.)

Stephen: I wish Father hadn't had to go off to Jerusalem to register for the Roman tax. And I wish he hadn't taken Eli with him.

(stands up, spreads his arms wide) Most of all, I wish something would happen around here. I can hardly stay awake.

(Ewe looks up at Stephen and bleats inquiringly.)

Stephen: *(insistently)* I mean it. I've never been so bored in all my life. Nothing to do here but watch sheep. *(looks down)* Nothing personal.

Ewe: *(shrugs, bleats)* I know something you don't know.

Stephen: What?

Ewe: *(bleats)* Uh-uh. *(shakes head no)*

Stephen: What do you mean, no?

Ewe: *(holds up hoof, bleats)* Wanna play?

Stephen: Play? You want to play?

Ewe: *(bleats)* Yeah.

Stephen: Oh, all right — there isn't anything else to do. *(stands up, starts to sing.)*
　　We are gonna play Ewe's clues,
　　We are gonna play Ewe's clues,
　　We are gonna play Ewe's clues,
　　'Cause I'm *really* bored.

(Ewe eyes Stephen, bleats accusingly.)

Stephen: *(sighs)* Okay. *(sings)*
　　We are gonna play Ewe's clues,
　　'Cause it's really *fun.*

(Ewe bleats with satisfaction and ambles away.)

Stephen: *(sings)*
    Now to play Ewe's clues,
    You've got to find the hoofprint
    'Cause that's the first clue,
    Then you write it on your scroll,
    'Cause they're whose clues?

Sheep: *(bleat)* Ewe's clues.

Stephen: *(looks around)* Now — did you see which way Ewe went?

Sheep: *(bleat)* That way!

Stephen: *(looks off into distance)* That way? *(sighs)* Okay. *(sings as he walks)*
    We are looking for Ewe's clues,
    We are looking for Ewe's clues,
    We are looking for Ewe's clues,
    Wonder where she's gone?

(Ewe comes upon a pair of Hay Bales and stamps one with a hoof, leaving an inked hoofprint. Ewe continues on with Stephen and the Sheep coming up a few moments behind her.)

Sheep: A clue, a clue!

Stephen: *(looks around in confusion almost on top of the Hay Bales)* Where? Where?

Sheep: Right there.

Stephen: Wha —? Where? Oh — there. *(leans over to inspect the marked Bale)* You're right, it's a clue, right on this here hay bale. *(touches the hoofprint)* Hello there, Hay Bale.

Hay Bale 1: Hello there, Stephen!

Stephen: *(does a double take)* Well — I didn't expect that.

Hay Bale 1: *(flaps arms)* Didn't expect what? That I would talk to you?

Stephen: Well — yeah.

Hay Bale 1: Who wouldn't talk with everything that's going on tonight?

Stephen: What do you mean? What's going on?

Hay Bale 1: *(disbelieving)* You don't know? *(looks at Hay Bale 2)* Can you believe it? He doesn't know! He must be slow.

Stephen: Slow? What did I miss? And why am I taking grief from a bale of hay?

Hay Bale 2: Don't feel bad, kid, he gets that way when he gets excited. This is a really big night, and we've got a lot to do.

Stephen: Are either of you going to tell me what's going on?

Hay Bale 1: Sorry, we've got to get to Bethlehem. There's somebody very special there that we have to keep warm.

Stephen: Somebody — what? Who?

Hay Bale 2: Sorry, kid, but we gotta bail. *(flaps arms)* Get it? We gotta *bail*.

Stephen: *(confused)* But —

(Hay Bales walk away quickly.)

Hay Bale 2: *(to Hay Bale 1)* I guess you were right, he really *is* slow —

15

(Stephen looks after Hay Bales as they waddle away.)

Stephen: Well, that certainly was strange. But it was our first clue, so we have to put it in our — *(pauses)*

Sheep: *(bleat)* Scroll.

Stephen: Right, our scroll. *(takes out scroll and quill, and speaks as he writes)* So our first clue is a hay bale. Now what do you suppose a hay bale would be a clue to?

(Sheep bleat noncommittally.)

Stephen: I know — I don't know, either. So I guess we have got to look for the second clue.

Congregation sings "Away In A Manger"

Stephen: *(sings softly, as he walks around the stage)*
   We are looking for Ewe's clues,
   We are looking for Ewe's clues,
   We are looking for Ewe's clues,
   'Cause it's lots of fun.

(Ewe has trotted ahead of Stephen, and leaves a hoofprint on Donkey's flank. Stephen walks past Donkey.)

Sheep: *(bleat)* A clue!

Stephen: *(looks at Donkey)* Did you say something?

Donkey: *(brays)* You talkin' to me? *(looks around warily)* Are you talkin' to me? I don't see anyone else here, so you must be talkin' to me.

Stephen: Yes, did you say something?

16

Donkey: Heck no. I'm too tired to talk.

Stephen: Then who —

Sheep: *(bleat)* A clue, a clue!

Stephen: Oh, you're right — *(leans over to examine the hoofprint on Donkey's flank)* — it is a clue. Right here on this here donkey. *(reaches out to touch hoofprint)*

Donkey: Hey, hey — watch where you're puttin' that hand, shepherd boy!

Stephen: *(snatches hand back)* Sorry, Donkey. I just noticed this hoofprint, here on your —

Donkey: Yeah, I wanna talk to you about that. Is that sheep yours? She's got no right to go around stamping her hoof on everything in sight.

Stephen: Sorry, Donkey, I'll talk to her about that. It's just a game, she didn't mean any harm.

Donkey: *(wearily)* Sorry, shepherd boy, I just got back from Bethlehem and I'm a little tired. I had to carry this pregnant woman from Nazareth to Bethlehem, and when we got there we found out they hadn't made a reservation! Can you imagine — all that way, and when they got there, they had no place to stay? I schlepped that woman all over Bethlehem, trying to find a bed —

Stephen: I'm sorry to hear that, Donkey. What happened to them?

Donkey: Oh, they found a place, eventually, I guess. Some innkeeper found them an empty stall in his stable. It's a good thing, too, because I think she was going to have the baby tonight.

Stephen: A stable? Wow, that's not much of a place to have a baby, is it?

Donkey: Hey, hey, speak for yourself, shepherd boy. Where do you think I was born, Jerusalem General Hospital?

Stephen: Yes, but you're a — *(hesitates)*

Donkey: Yeah?

Stephen: Oh, never mind. Go back to sleep, Donkey.

Donkey: *(walks away shaking his head)* A donkey can't get a decent night's sleep anywhere, these days.

Stephen: Hmmph. I guess Donkey is feeling a little grumpy tonight. But he's our second clue, so we've got to put him in our —

Sheep: *(bleat)* Scroll!

Stephen: *(whips out scroll and quill)* Right! Our handy dandy scroll. So now, we put a donkey —

Congregation sings "The Friendly Beasts"

(As the song is sung, all three Magi walk to center stage and stand looking up at the sky. Ewe sneaks up to Magi 3 and stamps a hoof-print on him, then sneaks away. Magi 3 looks around, but does nothing. The Magi look at the sky as Stephen walks around stage.)

Stephen: *(sings)*
    I just want to find Ewe's clue,
    I just want to find Ewe's clue,
    I just want to find Ewe's clue,
    'Cause I'm really *cold.*

(Stephen meets the Magi; they nod politely, he nods, and passes by without looking at the hoofprint on Magi 3.)

Sheep: *(bleat)* A clue, a clue!

Stephen: Why don't I ever see these things? *(looks around)* Where?

Sheep: *(bleat)* There! On that man!

Stephen: What man? Oh — here. *(approaches Magi 3)* Uh — excuse me, sir?

Magi 3: *(looks at Stephen, then back up at the sky)* What, young man?

Stephen: Uh — excuse me, but I just noticed you have a hoofprint, right there.

Magi 3: What? *(looks at hoofprint on robe)* Oh, that. Yes, there was a sheep a few minutes ago. I didn't see where it went. We're too busy. *(looks up at sky again)*

Stephen: *(looks up at sky)* Oh. What are you looking for?

Magi 3: A star.

Stephen: A star? There must be a million of them up there. Just pick one.

Magi 2: Not just any star.

Magi 1: A very *special* star.

Stephen: *(looks up again)* What kind of star? You mean, like a famous singer — *(sings)* Regrets, I've had a few, but then again —

Magi 3: *(impatiently)* Not that kind of star. A star in the sky.

Stephen: Oh. *(pauses)* I don't get it.

Magi 3: We're wise men, my friends and I. We know much about the world, and we know that tonight there is supposed to be a very special star in the sky.

Stephen: What makes it so special?

Magi 3: It's the sign that a great king has been born.

Stephen: A great king? *(excitedly)* That's exciting! That's wonderful! Where is this star?

Magi 3: *(points to stage left where the spotlight shines)* Right there.

Stephen: *(peers intently)* Wow!

Magi 3: *(looks at Stephen)* Do you see it?

Stephen: *(shakes his head reluctantly)* No.

Magi 2: Right *there*. The very bright star, with the tail.

Stephen: Ohh — *now* I see it. But there must be some mistake.

Magi 1: Mistake? We don't make mistakes.

Stephen: But that star — if it's supposed to mark the birthplace of a great king, it can't be that one. Jerusalem is that way *(points in a different direction)*. That's where the king would be. That can't be the star.

Magi 1: Well, it is.

Stephen: But —

Magi 3: My young friend, this is a very special star, to mark the birth of a special kind of king.

Stephen: I don't understand.

Magi 3: You will. Now we must go to visit this king. We have gifts. *(points to Magi 1)* Gold *(points to Magi 2)*, frankincense, and myrrh. *(as Magi start to walk toward the star, Magi 3 stops and turns to Stephen)* Off that way — what town lies there?

Stephen: *(shrugs)* Bethlehem is the closest town, I guess. But it's not much of a town.

Magi 3: *(over his shoulder as he walks toward Bethlehem)* It's not the town we're going to see, young man. It's the King.

Stephen: This is a very strange night. But you know what this means? We've got the third clue! *(takes out scroll and quill)* We've got three wise men, a donkey, and a bale of hay. What do you suppose that means?

(Sheep bleat noncommittally.)

Stephen: If we just had one more clue —

(The stage is filled with light, and Stephen looks up, drops his scroll and quill. Sheep look up, and stare.)

Stephen: Angels!

Congregation sings "Joy To The World"

Stephen: Wow, I've never seen anything like that, have you?

(Sheep bleat wonderingly.)

Stephen: *(sings)*
  We just got a message,
  We just got a message,
  We just got a message,
  Wonder what it means.

Old Shepherd: *(walks onstage, from the direction of the angels)*
Did you see the angels, Stephen? Did you see them?

Stephen: We sure did. We were just trying to figure out what they meant.

Old Shepherd: Don't you know? It's the fulfillment of the ancient prophecies.

Stephen: What ancient prophecies?

Old Shepherd: That God would send a Savior to deliver his people from sin and death.

Stephen: A Savior?

Old Shepherd: A Savior. He is descended from the family of King David, and his name will be Jesus. He's come to save us all.

Stephen: And this Jesus was born in Bethlehem?

Old Shepherd: Yes.

Stephen: And he was born in a stable. With bales of hay to keep him warm.

Old Shepherd: Exactly.

Stephen: Oh, *now* I get it.

(Ewe has come up to stand next to Stephen. When he finally realizes what has happened, Ewe slaps a hoof against her forehead and shakes her head.)

Stephen: *(to Old Shepherd)* So where are you going now?

Old Shepherd: You heard the angels. I'm going to Bethlehem, to see the King. Would you like to come along?

Stephen: Would I? This is great! This is fantastic! Ewe, thanks for telling me about this!

Ewe: *(bleats)* You're welcome.

Old Shepherd: *(eyes Stephen suspiciously)* You talkin' to that sheep, son?

Stephen: Uh ... what sheep?

(They start toward Bethlehem; Ewe trips Stephen as they walk by.)

Stephen: *(sings as he walks)*
  We are going to see Jesus,
  We are going to see Jesus,
  We are going to see Jesus,
  Going to see the King!

(As the shepherds walk to Bethlehem, Ewe leaves a hoofprint on the rock where Stephen had been sitting then joins the shepherds.)

Congregation sings "O Little Town Of Bethlehem"

Narrator: I'll never forget what we saw that night when we got to Bethlehem. It was just a baby, a simple little baby, asleep in a manger full of clean hay. He certainly didn't seem like anything special, but I knew he was. The wise men were still there, and there were shepherds coming in from all over the countryside to see this little king. And his parents — his parents looked tired and a little bit scared, as though they didn't know what to make of it.

(Stephen walks back from Bethlehem and sits on his rock. Before he sits, though, he sees the hoofprint. As Narrator speaks, Stephen is sitting, thinking.)

Narrator: I thought about it a lot, that night, and the nights afterward, for a long time. You've got a lot of time to think when you're tending sheep. I wondered how this little child could possibly be a king and how he could possibly save the world from sin. What could he do that could possibly make a difference?

(Stephen leans over to look at the hoofprint again.)

Narrator: And I thought about the last clue Ewe left me: it had something to do with a rock. What could it mean? I thought about it for a long time, and then I eventually forgot about it for many years. Many, many years. Until I heard about this man Jesus, traveling throughout the countryside, preaching about God's love, and God's salvation. I remembered the baby, then, and I knew this had to be the same person. This truly was the king who was sent to save us — but I still didn't know how he would save us. And then the authorities executed him, like a common criminal, and I thought it was all over.

And that's when I finally understood about the rock. Because after they killed him I went to see his tomb — and the rock at the entrance was rolled away. The tomb was empty. This man Jesus had risen. Suddenly it all made sense. The prophecies were fulfilled. And that's why even now, as I start my own journey to tell people the good news of his resurrection, I still think back to that night so long ago, when it all began, when Jesus came to bring us life. You know, Jesus wasn't the only one born that night. I think I was, too.

Congregation sings "O Holy Night"

The End

24

CSI: Bethlehem

Characters (in order of appearance)
>Guardsman
>Captain Of The Guard
>Horatio
>Zachariah (the innkeeper)
>Guest 1
>Guest 2
>Guest 3 (woman)
>Guest 4 (child)
>Innkeeper's Wife
>Lydia
>Artemis
>Esther
>Mary
>Nehemiah
>Shepherd 1
>Shepherd 2
>Eldest Daughter
>Angel
>Messenger
>Balthasar
>Melchoir
>Gaspar

Costumes

All characters wear appropriate costumes for the time period 2,000 years ago. Horatio needs some kind of CSI badge affixed to his breastplate.

Props

>Theme music from *CSI: Miami*
>Small table
>Rough bed

Pile of rags
Yellow caution tape or police tape
Pencil
Front desk
Chairs
Scrolls
Scraps of cloth
Tweezers
Plastic bag (used as evidence bags)
Sunglasses
Bale of straw
Floor debris
Lantern
Manger
Cloth strip
Three shepherd's crooks
Spear
Spotlight
Tent
Fire pit
Sword

Prologue

(The scene opens on a sparsely furnished room at the Bethlehem Inn. There is a small pile of rags center stage, toward the rear, a small table, and a rough bed. There is yellow caution tape across the entrance to the room, and Guardsman stands to one side. Captain Of The Guard and Horatio walk onstage; Guardsman lifts the tape so they can step under it.)

Captain Of The Guard: We think this is where they were.

Horatio: *(takes off cloak, hands it to Guardsman; "CSI" is emblazoned on the back of his breastplate.)* Did your men touch anything?

Captain Of The Guard: No, sir. Once we saw there was no one here, we sealed off the room and called for you.

Horatio: Good work, Captain. Just as you've been told. *(examines the table)* Have you talked to the innkeeper?

Captain Of The Guard: *(shrugs)* He's not much help. He's had hundreds of people through here in the last few weeks. The census, you know.

Horatio: Well, we know plenty of ways to improve his memory.

Captain Of The Guard: He seemed pretty nervous, so he might remember something when you talk to him. He couldn't even remember if there were young children in this room.

Horatio: *(stoops down near the pile of rags)* He couldn't, could he? *(looks up)* Smell that?

Captain Of The Guard: *(wrinkles his nose)* Yes. What —

Horatio: *(pulls out a pencil and starts to poke through the pile of rags)* Let me tell you, once you've smelled that odor, it's with you for life. You never forget it. *(continues poking, stops and peers at the pile)* You're not a family man, are you, Captain?

Captain Of The Guard: Me, sir? Never wanted to be. I've got enough of a headache looking after my men. Children give me the willies.

Horatio: Then you wouldn't know. But just for the record, this *(pokes into rag pile with his pencil, lifts out a cloth on the end of it, holds it up toward the soldiers)* this is what you've been missing.

Captain Of The Guard: *(covers his nose; Guardsman covers his nose also)* Sir?

Horatio: It's swaddling clothes, Captain — soiled swaddling clothes. *(drops the rag after a moment, stands up and wipes his hands)* And you know what they say ... where there's a dirty diaper, there's a baby. The innkeeper was lying to you, Captain. *(takes out a pair of sunglasses, puts them on dramatically)* Anyone with a nose would have known there was a baby in this room. And we're going to find him.

Prologue ends

(CSI: Miami theme song, "Won't Get Fooled Again" — comes up as Prologue ends. Horatio and the Captain walk offstage as Artemis, a CSI, enters the room and starts examining the floor and furniture.)

Scene One: The Innkeeper
(The scene opens at the front desk of the inn, which is just off the room in the Prologue. A small group of people is sitting to one side, under the supervision of a Guardsman, as Horatio and the Captain enter. Lydia, a crime scene investigator, is examining scrolls while Artemis is gathering evidence in the other room, including scraps of cloth and scrapings from the floor, which he puts into small bags.)

Captain Of The Guard: These are the people who were here when we arrived.

Horatio: Let's see if we can wrap this up quickly. *(to group)* I understand one of you is having some short-term memory problems. Which one of you is Zachariah, the Innkeeper?

Zachariah: *(pauses, then slowly rises, speaking wearily)* I'm Zachariah, the innkeeper.

(Another man pushes him to the side, steps in front.)

28

Guest 1: No, *I'm* Zachariah.

Guest 2: *(jumps to his feet)* No, *I'm* Zachariah.

Guest 3: *(pushes to the front)* *I'm* Zachariah.

Guest 4: No, *I'm* Zachariah.

(Horatio turns to look at the Captain Of The Guard, who shrugs.)

Captain Of The Guard: They're a feisty bunch.

Horatio: So they are. *(to the group)* Well, before we go on, let me tell you that the Zachariah *I* want to speak to is suspected of having lied to King Herod's guard. If we find that to be the case, he is going to be doing some serious dungeon time with some very large men with very bad attitudes.

(As Horatio finishes, the guests discreetly step back, leaving Zachariah standing by himself.)

Guest 1: Uh — that would be *him*. *(points to Zachariah, and sits down nervously)*

Horatio: Thank you. *(to Zachariah)* You're the innkeeper?

Zachariah: Yes, sir.

Horatio: Do you run the inn by yourself?

Zachariah: Yes, sir.

Innkeeper's Wife: *(stands)* I run it with him. *(pauses)* I'm his wife.

Horatio: I see. Nice of you to stand with your husband, considering. *(pauses)* As you know, we're looking for families with young children. We're *here* because somebody told us that they saw a baby right here, not long ago. What can you tell me about that?

Zachariah: You know what it's been like for the last couple of months, with the census. We're just five miles from Jerusalem, so we not only have all of the families from the house of David returning here to be counted, but all the tourist trade for Jerusalem, too. Nobody wants to pay what they charge at the inns there, so they try to get a room here.

Innkeeper's Wife: It's been madness. More families than we have rooms, more people than we have beds, more hungry mouths than we have food to give them. It's madness — I haven't had a good night's sleep in weeks.

Guest 2: Neither have I. I've been sharing a room with my husband and two goats. I'm not sure who smells worse.

Horatio: *(to Guest 2)* And what, exactly, did that add to this conversation? If you're that anxious to talk, we'll get to you later. *(to Zachariah)* So that's pretty much what you already told the good Captain, here.

Zachariah: Yes, sir. It's the truth.

Horatio: Yes, but is it the *whole* truth? *(Zachariah starts to speak; Horatio cautions him to be quiet with a raised finger)* Captain, you're a student of human behavior — did you notice anything about what this gentleman just said?

Captain Of The Guard: No, but he's sweating like it's the middle of summer.

Horatio: Good observation, but not what I'm looking for. Lydia, were you listening?

Lydia: Sure, H.

Horatio: And what did *you* notice about his answer?

Lydia: *(puts scroll down on desk)* That was no answer. He responded, but he never addressed your question.

(Zachariah dabs at his face and forehead with a rag; Innkeeper's Wife fidgets.)

Horatio: And what does that tell you?

Lydia: The same thing his guest registration tells me: He's lying.

Zachariah: *(blustering)* I am not —

Horatio: Let's hear the young lady out. Lydia?

Lydia: He's got guest registrations going back two months. About a week ago, on December 24, somebody signed in here *(holds up scroll)* but then it got crossed out.

Innkeeper's Wife: We must have found out there was no room in the inn after they registered.

Zachariah: It happens all the time. It's hard to know what's available when it's this busy.

Lydia: All the time? Really? *(holds up two more scrolls)* This is the registration for the next day. And this is the registration for three days later. The registration for December 26 is missing. Somebody's covering something up.

Artemis: *(stands up, with several scraps of cloth held in a tweezer)* Hey Lydia!

Lydia: Yes?

Artemis: Did you see any guests from Nazareth registered in the last week or so?

Lydia: No, why?

Artemis: Look at this material. It's a weave they use in Nazareth and the villages around it, and the wool is from a variety of sheep usually found in the hills there.

Horatio: So, Innkeeper, would you like to try it again — and actually answer my question, this time? Has there been a family with a child in this inn in the last couple of weeks — a family from Nazareth, perhaps?

(There is a long pause.)

Horatio: The evidence tells the story, Innkeeper. You're not doing yourself any favors.

Innkeeper's Wife: Tell him, Zachariah. It will be okay.

Zachariah: There was a couple. A young man and his wife, they couldn't have been more than twenty.

Artemis: From Nazareth?

Zachariah: Yes, yes, from Nazareth. *(Artemis pumps her arm victoriously)* They showed up on the evening of December 24. They'd been traveling all day and into the night. She was tired and pregnant. She looked like she was ready to give birth right then and there.

Innkeeper's Wife: She was in labor. She definitely was.

Zachariah: We had no room. We were booking families two to a room — there was nowhere to put them. But my wife felt sorry for them, and she let them register before I knew it. I crossed it out and told them we had no room in the inn.

32

Captain Of The Guard: And then?

Zachariah: I thought the man was going to cry. He didn't know what to do; he had nowhere to turn.

Innkeeper's Wife: The nights are cold this time of year. We couldn't very well let her have her baby in the street or off in some field somewhere.

Zachariah: So my wife thought of the stable, in the hillside just below the inn. It's not much, but it's warm and it's out of the wind. *(pauses)* We took them there, to the stable, and not much later we could hear a newborn child crying. A couple of days later that room over there opened up, so we let them have it.

Horatio: I see. *(pauses)* Zachariah, it sounds like you just might be telling the truth this time, so we're going to check your story. If it's true you may have saved yourself. If it's not —

Zachariah: It's true, it's true!

Horatio: For your sake, I hope it is. Captain, let's check out that stable. *(they start to walk away, Horatio hesitates and turns)* One more thing. Innkeeper. Why did you lie to the Captain?

Zachariah: Because we heard about what Herod's Guard was doing. This baby was harmless — he was no threat to anyone.

Horatio: That's not for you to decide, Innkeeper. Don't make a habit of lying, or you won't have a tongue to do it with.

(They start to walk away, leaving the Innkeeper dabbing sweat off his face.)

Captain: Do you really think this is worth our while? We're looking for a king, not a stable hand.

33

Horatio: King or stable hand, any child has potential — and, Captain, that's what we're here to guard against. *(puts on his sunglasses and strides out the door)*

Scene One ends

(Play theme song.)

Scene Two: The Stable

(The scene opens outside the stable. There is a manger, a bale of straw, and some other assorted debris on the floor. There are animal noises in the background as two criminalists — Esther and Mary — are examining the scene. Esther is examining the debris on the floor, Mary is passing a lantern over the manger and studying it closely. Horatio and Guardsman enter.)

Guardsman: ... so the bartender says, "I was talking to the *duck.*"

(Horatio smiles.)

Guardsman: You like that one?

Horatio: Not really. *(starts to enter the stable, pauses and looks back at Guardsman)* By the way, you may want to spend less time telling jokes and more time watching where you're going. There are donkeys here — and you just stepped in the evidence.

Guardsman: *(confused)* What? *(looks down at his feet, raises one sandal and looks at it)* Oh, man!

(He leans against the wall and raises his foot, starts to scrape the sole of his sandal with his sword. Horatio smiles, steps into the stable, where he looks around, then squats and looks at the floor.)

Horatio: So what do we have here?

34

Esther: There was definitely was somebody staying in this stable. *(puts something in an evidence bag, then stands up and points to the back of the stable)* There's remains of a fire, back there, and some food scraps.

Horatio: I see. Any idea how long ago?

Esther: Judging from the condition of the food scraps, I would guess not less than a week, and not more than two. The meat was pretty well gone, but the bones weren't completely stripped, and the bread was just starting to mold.

Horatio: How many people?

Esther: There are some makeshift pallets in the back, next to the cow stall. Pretty small — room enough for two people, if they were friends.

Horatio: Two people, eh? Look at the floor. It looks like there's been a small army through here. Sandalprints, bootprints, footprints ... and all since the last time it rained.

Esther: But still, there are just two sets of footprints back by the sleeping pallet.

(Guardsman finishes cleaning his sandals and ambles over to where Horatio and Mary are standing, where he stands by and listens.)

Horatio: Hmm. *(gestures to follow the path on the ground)* So they come in *here*, mill around *here*, and then they all seem to converge *here*. *(follows the prints over to the manger)* What do you find, Mary?

Mary: This manger is a treasure trove, H. Look here — this top layer of straw is recent. You can tell by fragments of straw, bitten in half, and the saliva all around the top layer. *(runs her fingers through the straw)* It's still wet, see?

Horatio: Interesting.

Mary: *(wipes her hand on Guardsman)* It gets better. *(scoops out straw and sets it aside carefully, on the ground)* Below the top layer of straw, there's a layer that's not as fresh — it's been in the manger for a while. Here we find this strip of cloth — it's a weave used in the region of Nazareth.

Horatio: Hmm. Just like the room in the inn.

Mary: And then there's this —

Guardsman: Ooh, what is this? Guacamole? *(dips a finger in, raises it to his lips)*

Mary: It's called meconium. It's the fecal matter excreted by newborn babies.

Guardsman: *(explosively)* Phtaah! *(wipes his hands on his tunic)* Ewww!

Horatio: So there was a newborn in this manger?

Mary: *(nods)* I'd say about a week ago.

Horatio: Hmm. And what's that smudge, there?

Mary: I don't know — let's see. *(leans closer, touches the straw, sniffs and tastes her fingertips)* Some kind of resin. Myrrh, I think.

Horatio: *(tests it himself)* Myrrh? That's used as a perfume, and as I recall, it's very expensive.

Mary: *(nods)* The last vial I bought cost me two weeks' pay.

Horatio: I hope it was worth it.

Mary: How do you think I got engaged? It's not because of the glamorous job I have.

Horatio: *(straightens up, looks around)* Something doesn't make sense, here. This couple is sleeping in a stable — they have their kid in a stable. Sounds like they don't have two shekels to rub together, but they can still afford something like myrrh. I don't —

(The Captain Of The Guard approaches, leading a group of civilians in simple robes, carrying shepherd's crooks. A guard with a spear is walking behind them, making sure they move along.)

Captain Of The Guard: *(interrupting)* Horatio! You have to hear this.

Horatio: *(irritated)* What? I was trying to figure out what these people were doing here. If we can figure that out, we can figure out who they were — and where they are now.

Captain Of The Guard: That's why you have to hear this.

Horatio: Okay, impress me.

(They crowd into the area at the front of the stable, while Horatio stands with his hands on his hips, looking unhappy.)

Captain Of The Guard: I had men on patrol outside the walls, looking for people who might be trying to slip out of the city. One of the patrols swept through a meadow north of town, then started to follow the main drag back into town —

Horatio: Are you getting paid by the word?

Captain Of The Guard: No, I'm getting paid to pay attention to what's going on around me. The patrol came upon these folks, here, headed *into* town. *(pauses) Nobody's* trying to get into Bethlehem, these days. Except them.

Horatio: Who are they?

(A Shepherd from the middle of the group steps forward.)

Nehemiah: We are shepherds, sir, from the hills outside the city.

Horatio: And you are?

Nehemiah: Nehemiah, of Bethlehem, sir, and these are my children.

Horatio: On your way to a family reunion, were you?

Nehemiah: No, sir. We were coming here to visit the stable.

Horatio: What stable?

Nehemiah: Why, this one, of course.

Guardsman: Why, are you running low on baby poo?

Nehemiah: We came to show my eldest daughter the place of the miracle.

Horatio: What miracle?

Nehemiah: She wasn't with us last week, so she didn't see. We thought she might believe, if she could see.

Horatio: See what? Believe what?

Shepherd 1: Believe the miracle that happened.

Shepherd 2: Believe that a great king was born last week, right here in Bethlehem.

Horatio: What are you talking about?

Eldest Daughter: They've been like this for a week.

Horatio: What do you mean?

Eldest Daughter: All this, you know, "We saw a miracle." I break curfew, and my dad doesn't even yell at me. I get home in the morning, and he's like, "You won't believe what we saw." I was like, okay, whatever.

Horatio: And what was it they saw?

Eldest Daughter: Cha, like I'm supposed to be listening? What planet are *you* from?

Captain Of The Guard: *(to Horatio)* This is why I don't have children.

Horatio: *(to the others)* Who can tell me what they saw?

Shepherd 1: We saw the new king.

Horatio: The king? *(pauses)* I'm guessing that would come as a surprise to Herod. You know — the *real* king.

Nehemiah: And yet, she speaks the truth. That's why we were bringing my daughter here, so she could understand.

(As the Shepherds are talking, Esther and Mary step around the manger and block off a part of the stable floor with the manger and their bodies.)

Captain Of The Guard: I told you you'd want to hear this.

Horatio: *(puts a finger to his lips)* Let them tell their story. Go ahead old man — tell me about this king and this miracle.

Nehemiah: It happened a little over a week ago — the night of December 24. We were in the fields, tending our sheep ... it was a cold night, with just a sliver of moon for light. Time was dragging heavily —

(As he begins his story, the other Shepherds step back away from the stable; some of them lie down, two stay standing. Nehemiah steps toward them, so he is among them when he finishes talking.)

Shepherd 1: Father, are you tired?

Nehemiah: Just thinking, son. I'm worried about your sister.

Shepherd 1: She'll be fine, Father. Why don't you let us take the watch?

Nehemiah: I'll stay up a bit longer. She should be back soon.

Shepherd 2: It's already an hour past her curfew.

(Shepherd 1 whacks him with his crook; Shepherd 2 rubs his shin as Shepherd 1 speaks.)

Shepherd 1: That Caiphas seems like a nice boy. I'm sure everything is fine.

Nehemiah: So am I. But just because I know the sheep are safe doesn't mean I don't watch over them.

Shepherd 2: Then you —

(A bright light suddenly envelops them, and a figure in white appears, starts walking toward them.)

Angel: Shalom! Peace be unto you!

(The three Shepherds stand close to one another; the ones who were sleeping wake up, but stay crouched on the ground.)

Nehemiah: Who — who are you?

Angel: Peace! I am an angel of the Lord — *(Shepherd 1 drops his crook)* — and I am here to bring you glad tidings of great joy.

Nehemiah: You're ... what?

Angel: Peace be with you! I am a messenger of the Lord your God, sent to tell you of promises fulfilled and prophecies accomplished this very night.

Nehemiah: What do you mean?

Angel: Shalom and Alleluia, the Messiah is born to you this night in the city of Bethlehem. Go now and see the fulfillment of God's word for man! Bring honor and glory to the new King of kings!

Nehemiah: This Messiah — he is in Bethlehem? Not Jerusalem?

Angel: Peace. Go now to the city of Bethlehem, to the inn by the west gate, and visit the stable there. Make haste, for the king awaits!

(The light goes out, Angel walks away, and Nehemiah steps back toward the stable; Shepherds follow.)

Nehemiah: And then there was a whole host of angels, all singing praises to the new Messiah. They were as plentiful as the stars in the sky, but each one shined like a sun. They sang, and then they were gone. And we ran here, to this stable.

Horatio: That's a very interesting story, shepherd. *(pauses)* I don't suppose you have any proof?

Esther: Uh — I think I may have it, H.

Horatio: What do you mean?

Esther: *(to Nehemiah)* May I see your foot, sir? *(puzzled, Nehemiah raises his foot)* The sole of your sandal, please. *(reaches for his foot and raises it high as she studies it carefully, looking between it and the floor several times; Nehemiah struggles to stay on his feet)* See this, H?

Horatio: *(leans closer to look)* What's that?

(Nehemiah falls; no one notices.)

Esther: See these marks, here and here, on the bottom of his sandal? They correspond with some of these footprints. *(points to floor)* There's at least a dozen sets of footprints, and I'd be willing to bet that some of them match up to the sandals these other shepherds are wearing. *(turns her head to speak to Nehemiah, realizes he is on the ground and lets go of his foot)* Sorry. Were there more of you that came here, that night?

Nehemiah: *(gets to his feet)* A few. All of us, here, were present that night, except for my daughter.

Horatio: Okay fine, that proves they were here. *(to Nehemiah)* But do you have any proof for the rest of your story? Where is the evidence?

Nehemiah: *(shrugs)* What would you have me show you? A feather from an angel's wing?

Horatio: A story without the evidence to back it up is just a story. *(to Captain Of The Guard)* They have nothing more to tell me, Captain. They seem harmless enough — just let them go. *(to Nehemiah)* There is nothing for you here. There's no king, no Messiah — just a story to pass a winter's night. Go back to your meadows, shepherd.

Nehemiah: But —

(Horatio dismisses them with a wave of his hand. Shepherds exit.)

Captain Of The Guard: Don't you find their story the least bit remarkable, Horatio?

Horatio: Remarkable? It's fantastic. These shepherds have too much time on their hands, worrying about visions and angels and kings born in stables. I don't have time for fairytales, Captain. Herod has tasked me with finding every child born in this city — I need results and evidence, not fables.

(A uniformed Messenger hurries up to them and salutes the Captain.)

Messenger: Begging your pardon, sir, but you need to come quickly.

Captain Of The Guard: What is it, son?

Messenger: The travelers we thought had skipped town — a patrol has found them encamped not far from here.

(There is a moment of silence and then they all leave hastily in the direction from which Messenger came.)

Scene Two ends

(Play theme song.)

Scene Three: The Camp of the Magi

(The setting is the Magis' camp. There is a tent set up toward the rear, a fire pit is set up near the front, and the Magi are seated behind it, seemingly unconcerned. Guardsman is standing over them, not quite threatening them. Horatio and Captain Of The Guard enter the camp; Horatio gestures for Guardsman to leave.)

Horatio: So, you are the Magi — the wise men who sent King Herod into a tailspin and started all this.

(The center Magi — Balthasar — stands and bows slightly.)

Balthasar: Guilty as charged, sir.

Horatio: I wouldn't throw that word around quite so easily, wise man. King Herod was less than happy with the fact that you seem to have run out on him.

Balthasar: And yet, here we are. We've run nowhere, sir.

Horatio: Perhaps you should. Cooperate with us and I can make your lives easier.

Balthasar: *(sits)* Go on.

Horatio: I don't know what exactly you told Herod, but whatever it was it has certainly put him on edge. I gather you told him that some kind of royal heir had been born around here, a king?

Melchior: Not *a* king, young man, *the* king. The Messiah.

Horatio: Ah, there's that word again. Messiah. Can you tell me what it means?

Melchior: Ancient Hebrew texts and prophecies foretold a Messiah — a Savior of the Hebrew people, a king who will set them free and never let them be enslaved again.

Horatio: *(nods)* Hmm. Sounds like a pretty big job.

Melchior: The biggest.

Horatio: Hmm. Now, I don't know how things are back where you come from, but around here kings tend to run in families, and royal

44

families tend to live pretty well. *(pauses)* Can you tell me why a royal family would be sleeping in a stable? Because it seems there was a child born in a stable about a week ago, and a bunch of shepherds decided to give their sheep a rest and come pay their respects to the new Messiah — in a cave. Does that sound right to you?

Gaspar: The Messiah is not like any other king. We have no way to know what is right or wrong where he is concerned. Since this has never happened before, there is nothing to judge him against. He doesn't care what mortals think — he does what he must do, and we must accept it. We are his subjects.

Horatio: Well, maybe *you* are, but King Herod is still signing my checks. I think you're talking in circles because you don't know what to think. You saw some kind of sign in the sky and dragged your sorry carcasses halfway around the world expecting to see some great king — and when you got here, there was nothing of the kind.

Gaspar: Is that so?

Horatio: I believe it is. And that's why you don't want to go back and face King Herod, because you're going to look like three stooges. You may be men of great learning back where you come from, but here we deal in facts and reality. There is no Messiah. There is no new king that will save the world. Those are facts. Everything else is gibberish.

Gaspar: Is it so hard for you to believe prophecy?

Horatio: Prophecy? You want prophecy. I have a prophecy for you. *(draws his sword; Captain Of The Guard steps toward him; the Magi look on impassively as he raises it high in the air)* I prophesy that when I let go, this sword will fall to the ground. *(lets go; and it clatters to the ground) That's* prophecy — using your reason to predict the future — using evidence to construct a hypothesis.

Gaspar: *(picks up the sword)* Do you know why it fell?

Horatio: It's in the nature of things to fall when they're not supported. Anyone with eyes can see that. Anyone with an unclouded mind can understand it.

Gaspar: *(hands the sword back)* Then you believe in a power that can't be seen, a force that can't be touched by human hands. God created that force — is it so hard to believe there may be other forces out there, just as powerful, that you can't touch, or measure — or prove?

(Captain Of The Guard steps over to the other side of the camp, looks around curiously as Horatio speaks. At one point, he raises his head and sniffs.)

Horatio: Gibberish. Superstitious nonsense. If this is what passes for great learning in the East, we have nothing to fear here.

Gaspar: You have nothing to fear from us, in any case. We are scholars, Horatio. The only thing you need to fear is your own arrogance.

Horatio: *(sarcastically)* Really?

Melchior: Really. You are so willing to believe that the world around you is all that exists, and that what happens in this world can be studied and categorized and understood completely. You believe in this world so much that you're unwilling to even entertain the possibility that there is something more to existence, something more to this life.

Horatio: I think I've wasted enough time. I have my evidence, I know what happened.

Melchior: And what is that?

Horatio: A peasant couple had a baby. They were so poor, so inconsequential to this world, that they couldn't even find a room on the night she gave birth, so she had the child in a stable. At the same time, a trio of fuzzy-minded old scroll worms saw some strange light in the sky and decided that it was a sign from their God, so they followed it to Bethlehem, and discovered their "king" was just a baby in a manger. They were too embarrassed to tell King Herod what they found, so they decided to slink back home and hope everyone just forgot about it. On the way, they encountered some shepherds and shared their fantastic story. The shepherds dressed it up even more, to make themselves feel more important. *(pauses)* I think that sums it up pretty well.

Melchior: I suppose it does, in that tight little world you live in.

Horatio: The same world we all live in, old man. Some of us just see it with a little more focus than others.

Melchior: *(smiles slightly)* I suppose so. But the wise man knows the difference between focus and narrowness of vision.

Horatio: And the *wiser* man knows when his time is being wasted. *(to Captain Of The Guard)* Are you coming?

Captain Of The Guard: In a minute.

(Horatio shrugs and starts to walk away. Balthasar calls to him.)

Balthasar: Horatio!

Horatio: What is it?

Balthasar: Let me ask you this. Suppose the God who created all was watching us and he saw that we were enslaved by sin, sunk so deep into the superficial, physical world around us that our souls couldn't breathe. Then suppose he sent a deliverer, a Messiah who could lead humankind out of that snare, and the Messiah was born

47

to a humble couple, in a humble place — born as a common man, so he could live among common men, walk with them, and live their lives so that they would know he knew them. When the time came for this Messiah to lead his fellow man to salvation, don't you think they would trust him more, knowing that he had been one of them?

Horatio: *(after a moment's pause)* Nice story, old man. You just keep dreaming. I'm comfortable living in the real world.

Balthasar: And a bird is comfortable eating the bait, 'til the snare closes.

(Horatio dismisses Magi with a wave of his hand and walks away. There is a moment of silence before Captain Of The Guard speaks.)

Captain Of The Guard: Do you really believe the child in the stable was this Messiah?

Melchior: The prophecies foretold his coming, and the stars in the sky told us when and where. The child was born in the City of David, and angels came to sing his praises. Yes, I believe he was the Messiah. *My* evidence convinces me.

Captain Of The Guard: *(smiles)* It's all about the evidence, isn't it? *(takes a step or two away from the camp, then turns back.)* Speaking of evidence —

Gaspar: *(guarded)* Yes?

Captain Of The Guard: Whatever it is you're cooking smells very, very strong. But when I moved upwind, I discovered something else.

Gaspar: Really?

Captain Of The Guard: Really. Not long ago, my friend there told me that you never forget that odor once you've smelled it — and he's right. *(pauses)* I know there's a baby in the tent, back there. After I'm gone, tell the parents it will be safe for them and their baby to leave at dawn tomorrow. Herod is still on a rampage, and the roads north and west are being patrolled, but they can still make their way south toward Egypt. *(smiles again)* I happen to know that the patrols will be pulled from that road tomorrow morning.

Gaspar: *(relieved)* Thank you. I understand.

Captain Of The Guard: You know — I think I'm starting to understand, too. This God you talk about must love us a lot — I guess it's only fair to love him back.

(Captain Of The Guard walks away, and Magi look after him for a moment, then Gaspar goes back to the tent and slips inside.)

The End

COPS: Bethlehem

Characters
(in order of appearance)
Benjamin
Cameraman (nonspeaking)
Producer
Extras (nonspeaking, people used in crowds)
Street Person 1
David
Innkeeper's Wife (Martha)
Innkeeper (Ezra)
Angry Mob 1 (part of the angry mob)
Angry Mob 2 (part of the angry mob)
Angry Mob 3 (part of the angry mob)
Joseph
Ezekiel
Ezekiel's Wife
Melchior
Balthasar
Gaspar
Passerby (woman)
Shepherd 1
Shepherd 2
Shepherd 3
Mary

Costumes
All characters wear appropriate costumes for the time period, 2,000 years ago.

Props
2 sets of police gear (helmets, badges, belts, spears, plastic handcuffs)

Video camera (an old VHS camera is good, but a camera can
   also be made from a shoebox)
Boom microphone (microphone attached to a broomstick or
   other pole)
Scrolls
Pouch with drawstring
Inn furniture
Camel
Small lamp
Small flask
Coins
Basket
Three shepherd's crooks
Manger
Doll (baby Jesus in manger)

Scene One: The Inn

*(Scene One opens on the streets of old Bethlehem with two officers
on foot patrol. A Cameraman and Producer are following the officers, and the senior officer is talking to the camera as they walk.
People are milling around the street as they walk by.)*

Benjamin: Anyway, this time of year you see a little bit of everything, no matter what. The harvest is in, it's too early to plant for
next season, so you've got people with time on their hands. People
plus spare time always equals trouble.

Producer: Like what kind of trouble?

Benjamin: Usual sort of stuff, in a city like this. Pickpockets, char-
latans, the occasional mugging, some scam artist trying to get your
help to transfer money out of a bank account in Ethiopia. Everybody has an angle.

Street Person 1: *(steps in front of them, holds up a scroll)* Got your map of the Prophets' Tombs, right here. Ten shekels. It's the only one of its kind, only one copy made — drawn by a scribe who was struck by blindness the day he finished it.

Benjamin: Really?

Street Person 1: *(glances anxiously at camera)* Really. Best bargain you'll ever see, Captain. For you, eight shekels. I've always been partial to the boys in blue, Captain.

Benjamin: It's Sergeant.

(As they talk, David, the other cop, reaches out and slips a pouch off the street person's shoulder, dumps out a dozen identical scrolls.)

David: One of a kind? What are these?

Street Person 1: *(looks down at them, wide-eyed for a moment, then drops to his knees and throws up his hands)* It's a *miracle!* Praise the Lord!

David: *(kicks the scrolls aside)* Get on with you, before I show you the Miracle of the Blunt Object.

(Street Person 1 scrambles to gather up the scrolls, stuffs them into the pouch and hurries offstage. David picks up one, studies it idly as the others talk.)

Benjamin: Of course, it's worse this year than it usually is.

Producer: Why is that?

Benjamin: The Roman census, of course —

David: *(interrupts)* Census! It's not enough that they enslave us, that they take away our freedom and desecrate our temple, but they have to make sure they have an accurate count of us so they know how much they can expect to steal from us every year. *(makes a spitting gesture)* Caesar Augustus can count my — oof!

(Benjamin elbows David, points over his shoulder to the camera and mimes using a movie camera. David falls silent.)

Benjamin: What I think my young friend was getting at is that there have been some problems with the census. It's caused a lot of hardship in the last month or so, for some folks.

Producer: Why is that?

Benjamin: Rome has ordered that everyone must go back to the ancestral home, the city where their family came from, to be counted.

(Innkeeper's Wife steps out into the street to flag them down.)

Innkeeper's Wife: Watchmen! Watchmen! Can you hurry, please? I think there's going to be trouble!

(The entourage of officers and journalists hurry to the door of the Bethlehem Inn where Innkeeper's Wife is waiting anxiously. They step inside. The inn is messy and there are four people standing at the desk.)

Innkeeper's Wife: Thank goodness you came! I was afraid things might get ugly.

David: *(looks around distastefully)* If that's what you were worried about, I'm afraid we're too late, ma'am.

Innkeeper's Wife: *(momentarily confused)* What?

David: Who did your decorating, the Goths?

Innkeeper's Wife: Don't worry about that, now —

David: You should really think about getting those *Trading Spaces* people to come here. They can do wonders.

Benjamin: Let the lady talk, David.

Innkeeper's Wife: You can see there's a crowd forming here. They're angry. It's an angry mob. Help us!

Innkeeper: *(embarrassed)* Now, Martha —

Innkeeper's Wife: It's an angry mob. Somebody's got to do something!

Angry Mob 1: You're darn right we're angry! We need a place to stay!

Angry Mob 2: We booked our room six months ago, and this innkeeper, here, is telling us he doesn't have a room for us! *(pulls out a scroll)* I have a confirmation number! I have a late check-in guarantee!

Angry Mob 3: And I have a confirmation, too! And a mother-in-law who's going to boil me alive if I don't have a room for her for the night.

Innkeeper: And I have no more room! I don't care what kind of paper you have, I can't just magically produce another wing on the inn. Have you been outside lately? Have you looked at the roads, and the streets, and the town well?

Angry Mob 2: *(waves scroll in Innkeeper's face)* What about my confirmation?

Innkeeper: *(snatches scroll from Angry Mob 2's hand and rips it)* What confirmation?

(Benjamin steps forward, carefully reaches out to put his spear between Innkeeper and the rest of the crowd.)

Benjamin: Okay, I think we need to take a step back, here. Let's everybody calm down a bit, take a deep breath, and try to work this out.

Angry Mob 1: He can work it out right now. Just give me my room! *(others say more or less the same thing. Benjamin turns to Innkeeper; Cameraman gets closer, Producer leans in with microphone.)*

Innkeeper: *(nervously)* That's what I've been trying to tell everyone. There is no room at the inn. I can't help them — nobody can. There's not a room to be had within a day's walk of Jerusalem. The only room we've got left is the stable, and even the animals are getting a little crowded.

Benjamin: Okay, what about doubling up? *(to the mob)* Would you be willing to share rooms?

Angry Mob 1: *(looks at Angry Mob 2)* I can't, with him. He's a Samaritan. No offense.

Angry Mob 2: *(points over his shoulder at Angry Mob 3)* And he's a tax collector. No one would stay with him. He's the reason we're in this mess.

Angry Mob 3: *(shrugs)* I just follow orders. Nobody likes paying taxes. I'd be willing to share, but my mother-in-law is kind of picky —

Innkeeper: It doesn't matter anyway. It's what I've been saying, there's just no room. We're already doubled up in the guest rooms, and I've got families sleeping in my lobby tonight. You're not going to be able to get up and go to the bathroom without stepping on someone during the night. I can't crowd anyone else in.

David: Sounds like a bad time for a visit from the Fire Marshal.

(Benjamin rolls his eyes, shakes his head.)

Innkeeper: Go ahead, shut me down. Then you're going to have ten times this many people screaming for a place to stay. I'll send them to your house.

Benjamin: Nobody's shutting anybody down. So you're saying you don't have any room — and you *(to the mob)* if he did have a room or two, that wouldn't do you any good, is that right? You all need separate rooms?

Mob: That's right.

Benjamin: Then here's what's going to happen. In about thirty seconds, I'm going to start taking people in for vagrancy. Anybody inside the city walls who doesn't have a room to sleep in is going to spend the night in the Jerusalem lockup. If they're lucky, they'll get to leave in the morning — but you never know, King Herod's jailers get a little overeager, sometimes, and someone might end up minus an eye or a limb, or something worse.

Angry Mob 1: Now look, let's be reasonable —

Benjamin: If you'd rather not gamble on how cranky the jailers might be, you can be outside the walls by the time I start rounding people up. There's shepherds out there, in the hills. Find a group of them and bed down for the night, and come back to be counted in the morning. Give 'em a few shekels, and you might get a place by the fire.

Angry Mob 2: Shepherds? Why would I want to spend the night with shepherds?

Angry Mob 3: Because you *don't* want to spend it in the lockup. Come on, let's go. I have to figure out how to explain this to my mother-in-law.

Angry Mob 1: Mother-in-law? Try explaining it to my wife. She hasn't been in a good mood since ... ever.

(Angry Mob leaves; Joseph remains behind. He had been standing behind the others, listening without speaking. He looks tired and a little afraid.)

Joseph: Uh — excuse me, sir ... you mentioned that you had room in the stable?

Innkeeper: I was being sarcastic. I can't rent you the stable, son.

Joseph: Normally I wouldn't ask, sir, but we really need a place to stay. My wife is with child — and I'm afraid the journey has been too hard on her, and she's going to have the baby *tonight*. She needs a roof over her head to do that.

Innkeeper: But I —

Innkeeper's Wife: Shush, don't be a hardheaded old man, Ezra. How far along is your wife, son?

Joseph: Eight or nine months, I think.

Innkeeper's Wife: Then it may well be time. We can put you up in the stable for the night, young man. It's the cave in the hillside, just south of here.

Joseph: *(anxiously)* Thank you! Thank you! Let me tell my wife! *(hurries out of the room)*

Producer: *(watches Joseph leave)* This is a nice thing you're doing. I'm glad we were here for it.

Innkeeper's Wife: *(shrugs)* I guess. We all do what we have to do. We're occupied, you know — we have to take care of one another.

Producer: Very nice. *(signals Cameraman to stop taping; they turn and start walking away)*

Innkeeper's Wife: *(as they walk away)* Besides, donkeys and cows don't pay rent. People do. Every shekel helps, you know?

(Producer looks back at her, then at Cameraman, who shrugs and indicates he's already stopped taping.)

Benjamin: *(shakes his head)* Like I said before, everybody's got an angle. Come on, it's time to check the watch at the gates.

(Benjamin and David walk off together with Producer casting one more backward glance at Innkeeper and Innkeeper's wife.)

Scene One ends

Scene Two: The Gate
(Scene Two opens as the Officers, Cameraman, and Producer are standing on a Bethlehem street, with Ezekiel and his wife, next to a camel. Ezekiel is in a sleeveless T-shirt and is trying to look unconcerned; his wife is nervous.)

Benjamin: So — *(looks at scroll)* — Ezekiel, is this your camel?

Ezekiel: Yeah, it's, like, totally mine, man.

Benjamin: *(hands scroll back to Ezekiel)* Could I see the registration, please?

Ezekiel: I — uh — I — I don't have it, man. I think I left it at home.

Benjamin: You wouldn't be driving an *unregistered* camel, would you? You wouldn't be trying to avoid the tax, would you?

Ezekiel: No, no, I'm good. I mean it, I'm good. I know I got it at home.

David: *(slowly walks around camel as he speaks)* Do you know why we pulled you over, Ezekiel?

Ezekiel: I don't know, man. I just know I'm gonna be late for work. Is this gonna take long?

Benjamin: You blew through a stop sign, back there a couple of blocks. Before that, you were going down the wrong side of Main Street.

Ezekiel: Wrong side? Man, isn't that a one-way street anymore? It used to be a one-way. *(agitated)* Look, man, I've got to get to work. I'm going to be late.

David: I think you need to focus, Ezekiel. This could be bad for you. *(whacks the back end of the camel with the butt of his spear, knocks off a small lamp; the camel snorts)* Look, Sarge — the taillight's broken.

Ezekiel: Look, what is this? What's going on here, man? You really gonna roust me for a lousy walking stop? I know what this really is! I know what this really is!

Ezekiel's Wife: *(takes his arm)* Ezekiel, don't get like that. Cool down! You can't afford to —

Ezekiel: *(shrugs off her hand)* Look, man, we all know the only thing I'm guilty of is DWG — driving while Galilean.

David: That's it! *(grabs Ezekiel)* Up against the camel! Feet back, hands on the hump. *(begins searching Ezekiel once he's in position)*

Ezekiel's Wife: *(upset)* I told you to calm down! I told you to take it easy!

Ezekiel: I didn't do nothin'! They just don't like us country people down here in the city. I didn't do nothin', man.

David: No? *(straightens up, holding a small flask pulled out of a pocket in Ezekiel's robe; passes it over to Benjamin)*

Benjamin: *(takes the lid off, sniffs it, dabs a finger in, and touches it to his tongue)* How long you been doing myrrh, son?

Ezekiel: I went to the dentist today, man! Got two teeth pulled out, and he gave me some myrrh to dull the pain. *(opens his mouth widely)* Want to see? *(opens mouth again)*

David: *(backs away)* Oh, man, you want to brush, or something? Something die in there?

Ezekiel's Wife: He really was at the dentist, officer. And he told him not to drive. I told him not to drive. But he wouldn't listen.

Benjamin: Dentist, eh? Well, until we get everything sorted out, you're going to have to go to lockup.

Ezekiel: Look, man, I'm already late for work. I've got to get the ovens fired up, or the bakers won't be able to do anything when they come in, in a couple of hours.

Benjamin: *(shrugs)* It wasn't my choice, it was yours.

(Ezekiel walks over to the line.)

Ezekiel's Wife: *(sobs)* I tried to get him to give me the reins, but he wouldn't do it. I tried!

Benjamin: You should have listened to your wife, Ezekiel. David, take him in — and take this along. *(hands him the flask)*

David: *(starts to put plastic cuffs on Ezekiel)* Ezekiel, you are under arrest. You have the right ... What am I saying, it's 4 BC — you don't have any rights. Just come with me.

Ezekiel: *(as David hustles him offstage)* I'm innocent! You can't do this to me! I'm going to be late for work!

Ezekiel's Wife: Ezekiel! I'll wait for you! Everything's going to be okay! *(to Benjamin)* What's going to happen to him?

Benjamin: He should be fine. He'll spend a night or two in the lockup, while we sort things out, but he should be fine unless King Herod takes a dislike to him. He's not related to the king, is he?

Ezekiel's Wife: Ezekiel? No, not even close.

Benjamin: Good, everything should be fine. You know, there's a saying that it's safer to be King Herod's pig than his relative. *(pauses, looks at camera)* Can you take that out?

Producer: All sorts of things end up on the cutting room floor, Benjamin. Just depends on how much interesting footage we get.

Benjamin: I'll try to keep the rest of the night interesting. *(to Ezekiel's Wife)* Are you okay, ma'am?

Ezekiel's Wife: I guess so. If I hurry, I can make it home before the kids wake up.

Benjamin: You left your children home — alone?

Ezekiel's Wife: *(shrugs)* We had things to do. The oldest is almost five — he can take care of things, if need be.

Benjamin: Then you'd best be getting along, ma'am. And drive safely. *(touches his helmet in farewell)*

(Benjamin, Producer, and Cameraman walk on as Ezekiel's Wife and camel move offstage.)

Benjamin: You know, in this job especially, you see so much wrong in the world. So many ways people screw up, so many ways people can make the wrong choices. *(glances back over his shoulder)* You look at someone, and you think to yourself, "How did they end up *here?*" Given a choice between right and wrong, how come we make the wrong choice so many times?

Producer: It's just the way people are, I guess. I see it, too.

Benjamin: I'm sure you do. I've been doing this since ... oh, since I was David's age, I suppose. And after all those years, I can't look back and say, "Well, things were bad then, but they've gotten better." People are doing the same things now they did then.

Producer: Is that why you stay in this? Are you trying to make things better?

Benjamin: I hope not — otherwise I'd be very depressed by now. I'm in it because this is what I know how to do ... and I keep hoping that something will come along that will make it better. Or at least give us reason to hope. When that happens, I want to be there.

Melchior: *(from offstage)* Excuse me, sir?

(Benjamin, Producer, and Cameraman stop, turn toward Melchior's voice.)

Melchior: *(hurries onstage, with Balthasar and Gaspar)* Excuse me, sir?

Benjamin: What can I do for you?

Melchior: I'm afraid we might be lost, and I'm hoping you can put us back on the right path. We're looking for a king.

Benjamin: Looking for a king? Then I *know* you're lost. Jerusalem is that way, about four miles. That's where you'll find King Herod's court. *(looks at them closely)* You're not from around here, are you?

Balthasar: We have come here from far away. I am Balthasar, a Royal Astronomer from Babylon. Gaspar is a scholar of ancient texts from the library at Ur, and Melchior, here, is a philosopher from the University of Babel. And it's not King Herod or his court we seek.

Benjamin: I thought you were looking for the king?

Balthasar: We are. But King Herod is the old king — we have traveled here looking for a new king, the one foretold by your own great prophets and proclaimed by the stars of heaven.

Benjamin: New king? I haven't heard of any births at the palace in Jerusalem.

Gaspar: The new king we seek will not come from the family of Herod. Your own prophets have foretold that he will come from the family of King David. It was Micah who said, "But you O Bethlehem Ephrathah, who are little among the clans of Judah, from you shall come forth for me one who is to be ruler of Israel."

Benjamin: *(looks around, tries to point subtly to the camera, which has closed in on them)* Look, Casper —

Gaspar: Gaspar.

Benjamin: Whatever. I don't know what the king is like back where you come from, but around here it's not too healthy to go talking about a new King of Israel that's going to replace King Herod. The man gets moody. You don't want to be on his bad side, even if you are from out of town.

Gaspar: We did not write the prophecy, my friend — we have only read it, and understood it.

Benjamin: He's not real big on reading and understanding, either. He's more into people just sitting down and being quiet. You don't want to be called to his court, Jasper.

Gaspar: Gaspar.

Melchior: In truth, sir, we have already been to visit your King Herod. We thought it best to announce ourselves when we entered his kingdom. We wanted to extend a hand of friendship from the East and pay our respects.

Balthasar: That, and some of his spies spotted us when we crossed the border.

(Melchior shrugs agreement.)

Benjamin: And he let you come looking for this new king, after all you told him?

Melchior: He seemed very eager for us to find him. He even asked that we go back to Jerusalem to let him know where this new king is, once we have found him. He said he wants to see this new king for himself, to pay his respects.

Benjamin: I'll just bet he does. So how can I help you? I still say if you're looking for a king, you're in the wrong place. We are just overrun with people right now — common people. Very common people.

Gaspar: And yet your prophets have told us the place, just as the stars have announced the date. He *is* here. Believe us.

Benjamin: Listen, Gaston —

Gaspar: Gaspar.

Benjamin: — take another look at the stars. There's thousands of them up there — it's easy enough to misread them, right?

Balthasar: Not really. We know it's now, we know he's here ... we just have to find him. Now, we thought we would start at the actual birthplace of your King David *(unrolls a scroll, holds it out for Benjamin to look at)*, and just inside the gates we met this very helpful young man who happened to have a map of famous sites from King David's time —

Benjamin: *(takes the scroll and looks at it, shakes his head)* Let me guess. You bought this from him, right?

Melchior: He didn't want to sell it, but we really needed it. Then he was going to give it to us, but we talked him into accepting payment for it.

Balthasar: It seemed only fair. It was a rare and valuable artifact, passed down in this young man's family for many generations ... we're lucky it was still in one piece.

Benjamin: In one piece? You're lucky the ink was dry. Look, Gaspar —

Gaspar: *(automatically)* Casper. *(does a double-take)*

Benjamin: The man's a scam artist, a hustler. *(hands the scroll back to Balthasar)* How much did he let you force him to take?

Balthasar: *(takes the scroll, looks at it dispiritedly)* A hundred shekels.

Benjamin: Whew! He sure had you pegged. Sorry to say, you've been had, friends.

Balthasar: He seemed so honest. We *trusted* him.

Benjamin: Listen, when you've been doing this as long as I have, you learn not to put your trust in anyone, or anything. They'll only end up letting you down.

Melchior: That seems like a lonely way to live, Sergeant. I've found that in the end, trust and faith are the only things you can count on — everything *else* will just let you down.

Benjamin: And here you are, 1,000 miles from home, with no place to lay your head, looking for a person no one knows.

Melchior: God never promised us an easy journey, Sergeant — just an interesting one.

(As they're talking, Street Person 1 wanders onstage, counting money. He stops when he realizes who else is there, and Balthasar makes eye contact first.)

Balthasar: That's him! That's the man who sold us the map!

(All turn to face Street Person 1.)

Street Person 1: Hey, I don't know what you're —

Benjamin: You! Hold it right there!

Street Person 1: (*realizing who Benjamin is*) Oh, man!

(*Street Person 1 takes off running. Benjamin takes off after him, with Cameraman and Producer close behind. The Magi watch for a moment, then follow.*)

Scene Two ends

Scene Three: The Stable
(*Scene Three opens on another street in Bethlehem. Benjamin, the Producer, Cameraman, and the Magi walk onstage from one direction, looking around.*)

Balthasar: I don't see him. I think we've lost him.

Melchior: How can that be? How can a man disappear into thin air?

Benjamin: When you live on the wrong side of the law, you become very good at hiding from it. You might even convince yourself you'll never get caught — but you can't hide from the law forever. Eventually, there's a reckoning.

(*Passerby walks onstage carrying a basket.*)

Gaspar: Excuse me, ma'am? Ma'am!

Passerby: (*stops*) What, me?

Gaspar: Yes, ma'am. Did you see a young man running down this street in the last couple of minutes?

Passerby: (*looks at the Magi*) I don't know. It's late, and I'm tired. My memory isn't very good, right now —

68

Balthasar: No? *(takes out a handful of coins, holds them out to the woman)* Perhaps this will help your memory.

Passerby: *(pleased, takes the coins)* Hmmm. Perhaps it will. Who were you looking for?

Balthasar: A man, running down this street within the last few minutes.

Passerby: About this tall *(shows height with her hand)*, dark hair, brown robe, running like Old Man Herod was chasing after him?

Balthasar: That would be him. Where did he go?

Passerby: Don't know, didn't see him. But thanks for the donation. *(walks off, laughing to herself)*

Benjamin: *(who had been watching skeptically)* I could have told you that would happen.

Melchior: Then why *didn't* you?

Benjamin: Because you're free to make your own mistakes. Free will, you know. But, look, you guys are going to have to be a little smarter about how you do things, or people around here are going to talk about you for a long time — about how not-very-bright you were.

Melchior: Then that's their right. Free will, and all. You can't live your life believing that everyone around you is a criminal.

Benjamin: Sure you can. And you'll end up being disappointed a lot less often. I —

(Benjamin is interrupted by the sound of sheep bleating. He pauses, looks around.)

Benjamin: Where is that noise coming from?

Balthasar: *(points)* Just outside the gate, I think.

Benjamin: Don't they know what time of the night this is?

(Shepherds walk onstage, followed by David and Ezekiel, still in cuffs. David and Ezekiel seem confused. The sheep continue to bleat occasionally.)

Shepherd 1: Excuse me, sir, but have you seen the new king?

Benjamin: New king? I think the guys you want to talk to are over there. *(points to the Magi)*

(The Shepherds walk past, David starts to walk by, also, but Benjamin catches him by the arm.)

Benjamin: David! What are you doing here? You should be in Jerusalem by now.

David: I — I don't know. Something incredible just happened.

Benjamin: What are you —

Ezekiel: *(animated)* It was awesome, man! It was, like, totally ... awesome!

Benjamin: Thank you, Mister Dictionary. Totally. David, snap out of it! What happened out there?

(Benjamin, David, and Ezekiel stop talking out loud, although they still seem to be speaking. The Shepherds are now speaking to the Magi, at the other side of the stage.)

Shepherd 2: Have you seen the new king?

Balthasar: No, we haven't. How did you come to know about the new king?

Shepherd 3: Do you know where the new king might be? We must find him.

Balthasar: We may be able to help you. But how did you find out about him?

Shepherd 1: We were in the field, in the hills not far from here. My brother and I, there, were asleep. We had drawn lots, and our cousin *(gestures toward Shepherd 3)*, lost, so he was the night watch.

Shepherd 2: I heard voices — it was the other officer and his prisoner. I turned over and paid no mind. And then it happened.

Shepherd 3: A man — or maybe it was a woman — a person suddenly appeared in the sky, floating up there among the stars. His face glowed, and he said, "Don't be afraid! I bring you glad tidings of great joy!"

Shepherd 1: The light woke us up — and the voice. It was like ... music.

Shepherd 2: And then he said, "A new king, a Savior, the Messiah, has been born to you this night in the city of Bethlehem."

Shepherd 3: "And you will know it is him because you will find him lying in a manger, wrapped in swaddling clothes."

(Shepherds and Magi continue to talk, but without sound. David, Benjamin, and Ezekiel begin speaking out loud.)

David: I let the water cup fall out of my hand — I just stood there, like a tree, barely able to look at this creature, but not able to turn away. And suddenly it was like daytime out there — like the sun had come to earth, and there were no shadows, no dark places in the entire world. Hundreds — maybe thousands of these creatures appeared in the sky.

Benjamin: *(doubtfully)* Hundreds? Thousands?

David: Were you that much more comfortable with just one glowing being hovering in the air above us? I tell you, there were thousands of them all of a sudden, like the heavens had opened up.

Ezekiel: And they said, like, "Praise God! Glory to God! Glory to God in Heaven — and, like, peace and good will on earth, to everybody." *(shakes his head)* It was awesome.

David: And then they were gone. The light faded, and I realized I couldn't see any of them. It was just the shepherds and us ... like before. Only not like before. Because everything is *different* now. Do you understand?

Benjamin: What are you talking about?

Ezekiel: The Messiah is here! The Messiah has been born tonight — right here!

Benjamin: *(to Ezekiel)* Did you use some more myrrh? *(to David)* Did he get the bottle of myrrh?

Ezekiel: The only thing I got was the message, man. I got the message.

(Benjamin, David, and Ezekiel stop talking out loud and the Magi and Shepherds begin speaking out loud again.)

Gaspar: Are you sure this new king is the Messiah?

Shepherd 1: All I know is that the angels told us a new king has been born tonight, in the city of Bethlehem.

Shepherd 2: Just as it was foretold in the Torah.

Shepherd 3: He has come to deliver us all. Just as it was written by the prophets.

(The Magi walk to where Benjamin, David, and Ezekiel are standing. The Shepherds follow.)

Melchior: Did you hear what happened? Did they tell you?

Benjamin: They told me. I just don't know if I believe it. Face it, I've got a myrrh-head and a young officer who seems to be in shock. Not your best witnesses.

Melchior: But we have three shepherds — and I'll bet you they told the same story.

Benjamin: No bet. Something happened out there — I'm just not sure what.

Balthasar: There's an easy way to find out. They were told to look for a baby, lying in a manger, wrapped in swaddling clothes.

Benjamin: Right, and what kind of sense does that make? Why would anyone have a baby and put it out in a stable ... *(slows down)* ... in a manger ... Oh my gosh.

Balthasar: What?

Benjamin: The Bethlehem Inn. It doesn't make sense — it doesn't make sense at all — but I think I saw them earlier tonight. The father, at least.

Producer: At the inn! The young man who asked if they could stay in the stable!

Benjamin: And he said his wife was about to give birth! Come on, the stable is over this way!

(The entire entourage moves across the stage to the setting of the stable. Mary and Joseph are sitting by a manger, in which rests a baby. Everybody hangs back for a moment or two, and then Melchior steps forward hesitantly.)

Melchior: Is this the child that we were told about?

Joseph: I suspect that he is.

Balthasar: And what will you call him?

Mary: *(reaches out to the manger, pats the baby)* We will call him Jesus.

Gaspar: And he will also be called Marvelous, Counselor, Prince of Peace, King of kings —

Mary: All in good time. But for tonight, he is Jesus. Our son.

Shepherd 1: And our Savior. *(kneels)*

Shepherd 2: Let us worship him. *(kneels)*

Shepherd 3: The ancient promise is fulfilled. *(kneels)*

(David takes off Ezekiel's cuffs, and they both join the Shepherds, kneeling. Gaspar and Balthasar give gifts to Mary and Joseph. Melchior and Benjamin step back, to speak.)

Benjamin: This is the Messiah? How can that be? The Messiah is supposed to be a great leader.

Melchior: Being born in humble circumstances doesn't mean that a child can't grow up to be someone truly remarkable — anymore than being born in a royal court means that a child will grow up to be a leader worthy of respect. It's not how you're born, or who you are born to — it's what you do with the life you are given that tells the measure of a man.

Benjamin: And that man — that child — in there?

Melchior: Is destined for great things. Great and terrible things. He is here to set us free.

Benjamin: From the Romans? *(looks over his shoulder at the camera, then back to Melchior then lowers his voice)* From King Herod?

Melchior: From ourselves. From the evil that we do. One day, that child in there will be a man, and that man will take on the sins of the world, so the rest of us can be free of the burden of what we have done.

Benjamin: But how?

Melchior: All in good time, son, all in good time. For today, let's just celebrate the fact that he is finally here. And tomorrow ... tomorrow is another day.

Benjamin: I told someone that I was waiting for things to get better, waiting for hope. I just never expected to find it ... not here, not tonight.

Melchior: The best gifts are always the ones we weren't expecting. *(puts an arm around Benjamin's shoulder)* Let's go in and see the future.

Benjamin: You know — I always wondered what the future would look like.

Melchior: The future has the face of a child, Benjamin, it always does. Just like hope.

The End

Trading Spaces: Bethlehem

Characters
(In order of appearance)
    Paige
    Simon
    Elizabeth
    Jacob
    Ruth
    Aaron
    Joseph
    Hildy
    Guard 1
    Melchior
    Guard 2
    Gaspar
    Balthasar
    Shepherd 1
    Jacob
    Shepherd 2
    Shepherd 3
    Shepherd 4
    Mary

Costumes
    Characters are dressed in costumes appropriate for the time period 2,000 years ago. Jacob and Ruth are dressed very plainly; Simon and Elizabeth are more fancily dressed. Aaron wears all black and Hildy wears flamboyant clothing.

Props
    Microphone
    Two sets of keys
    Table
    Chairs

Front desk
Fabric swatches
Shawl (for Hildy)
Brightly colored robe
Bowl
Clay pot
Small object
Coin
Ticket stub
Paper
Pencil
Bag of coins
Curtain

Prologue

(The Prologue opens with two couples and the host standing between them. One of the couples is very plainly dressed — simple shepherd-type clothing — the other is better-dressed, wearing brightly colored robes.)

Paige: Two rooms, two families, one weekend, and 500 shekels. This week's episode of *Trading Spaces* brings us to the little town of Bethlehem, just six miles from Jerusalem, where we're going to let the Simon family *(gestures to better-dressed couple, Simon and Elizabeth)* and the Jacob family *(gestures to plainly dressed couple, Jacob and Ruth)* spend one weekend totally remodeling a room in each other's home. Are you ready to go, Simon? *(extends microphone to Simon)*

Simon: Well, I —

Elizabeth: *(cuts in, taking over the microphone)* He's very excited to be here. We're both really looking forward to it!

Simon: *(shrugs)* What *she* said.

Paige: *(after a brief struggle for the microphone with Elizabeth)* How about you, Jacob?

Jacob: *(disgruntled)* I thought I was auditioning for *The Price Is Right.*

Ruth: *(leans in, apologetic)* It was the only way I could get him to put on clean underwear. He hasn't had much sleep. He's been working hard for the last few weeks, with all the people coming through here, and he won't hire any help —

Jacob: *(interrupts)* I'm not *made* of money, you know.

Paige: *(turns away, facing "camera")* And I'm sure it's a fascinating story, but we've only got an hour show, so there really isn't time for it. So, are you ready to ... trade spaces? *(crosses her arms to hold out keys to the two couples)*

Jacob: Do I have a choice?

Ruth: Not if you ever want to be happy again.

(Jacob takes the key reluctantly. In the meantime Elizabeth is practically jumping up and down in eager anticipation.)

Elizabeth: Come on, let's do it! Let's get this show on the road!

Simon: *(very low key)* Yee-hah. *(takes the key)*

Paige: That's the spirit. Now let's see what we have to work with.

(Theme music comes up; the couples walk offstage.)

Prologue ends

Scene One: The Inn

(Scene One opens with Paige walking to a simple room, furnished with a table, a couple of chairs, and a front desk. Aaron, dressed entirely in black, is standing in the center of the room, apparently studying the walls.)

Paige: Jacob and Ruth are proprietors of the Bethlehem Village Inn, where they are looking to have the common room remodeled. Ruth tells me it's been about ten years since anybody did *anything* to dress this place up. What do you think, Aaron?

Aaron: It's only been ten years? I haven't seen this kind of color scheme since Moses was a baby. Look at that. *(waves his hand toward the wall)* Can you believe it? And this floor — mud. Can you believe it? I mean, really. And don't get me started on this furniture. *(waves a hand around the room)* What is it, Early Palestinian Hideous?

Paige: So you, Simon, and Elizabeth have your work cut out for you.

Aaron: This may be the one the completely *ruins* my reputation. *(looks up)* And that fan has *got* to go —

Paige: *(makes a hurry-up gesture offstage)* Simon, Elizabeth, let's get in here and see what Aaron has in mind for this room.

Simon: Look, is this going to take long? I'm needed back at the palace. There's a delegation coming in from Babylon —

Elizabeth: *(hastily)* He doesn't mean it. He knows this is supposed to take the whole weekend. Don't you, dear? *(out of sight of the audience, she seems to be grabbing or poking him)*

Simon: Oww. Yes, right, all weekend. Just let me send a message to King Herod —

Aaron: Listen to me, dearie, the only message that you should be sending right now is SOS. This room is a *disaster*. So, since they won't let us burn this place down and start over, let's talk about color —

(Joseph enters the room hesitantly, walks up to the desk.)

Joseph: Excuse me.

Paige: *(startled)* Excuse *me*. We're shooting a show right now.

Joseph: What?

Paige: *Trading Spaces*? You know — two couples, two rooms, one weekend? *(Joseph stares at her blankly)* Don't you watch television?

Joseph: Sorry, no. I have a life. Can I get some help, here?

Elizabeth: Simon, why don't you take care of getting rid of this man, while we decide what to do with the room?

(Paige and Elizabeth huddle with Aaron as he starts pulling out swatches of fabric. Simon walks up to the desk, glad to be away from them.)

Joseph: Look, I know I was in here last night and you couldn't help me, but — say, you're not the innkeeper. What happened, did he finally fall over?

Simon: It's a long story. How can I help you, so we can get on with the show and get it over with?

Joseph: I was here late last night, and I talked to the innkeeper. What's his name?

Simon: Jacob.

81

Joseph: Right, Jacob. I talked to him last night about getting a room. My wife and I are here for the Roman census — we traveled all the way from Nazareth.

Simon: Right. There are many people on the move right now — this census is a nightmare. We've got people leaving their jobs, moving all over the place, and it seems like most of them are coming through here. And then they have to wait around to go through registration. It's going to cost King Herod a ton of money in taxes before it's all done. And the Romans don't care, as long as they get *their* taxes.

Joseph: I know it's bad, sir. This is the only inn in Bethlehem, and all of the rooms are full. I thought they might be able to make a space for us, somewhere, but the innkeeper said, "No." My wife and I slept in an olive grove outside of town last night.

Simon: Well, you have a lot of company, I'm sure.

Elizabeth: Simon, come here! You have to see the colors Aaron has picked out!

Simon: *(shrugs)* I'm sorry, but duty calls.

(Simon starts to turn away, but Joseph reaches out and grabs Simon's sleeve.)

Joseph: Sir! Please! My wife is pregnant — she's going to give birth any day now. She can't spend another night in the olive grove. She'll get sick — or the baby will.

Simon: I'm sorry, son, but if there aren't any rooms —

Joseph: There's only the two of us, sir. We don't need much room. We could sleep in the common room, here. In a corner. Just in the corner. That's all I ask.

Simon: *(looks around)* I'm sorry. We're remodeling this room this weekend, there's no way you can stay here. *(shrugs)* It's the wife's idea. She loves this show.

Joseph: *(lowers his head)* I don't know what I'm going to tell Mary. *(turns and starts to walk away)*

Simon: *(rubs his chin)* You — what's your name?

Joseph: Joseph. Joseph of Nazareth.

Simon: Well, Joseph, when we were riding up here, I thought I saw a little grotto in the hill below the inn. I think it's the stable for the inn.

Joseph: Yes?

Simon: *(spreads his hands)* If you're not too fussy, you could spend the night there. It's out of the wind and the cold, probably plenty of fresh straw you can use for bedding.

Joseph: *(thoughtfully)* A stable?

Simon: It's the only thing I can see. It's not the fanciest place on earth, but you could do worse. Actually, I think you've *done* worse.

Joseph: *(looks around)* Is it going to be okay with the innkeeper? He didn't seem like the most ... friendly person.

Simon: It'll be fine. He's gone for the weekend, off redecorating our bedroom at the palace. My room. *(shakes his head)* I don't know whoever thought of this. But you've got the weekend, at least. With luck, you may be able to register with the Romans by Monday.

Joseph: Then thank you. Thank you very much. Mary's going to be happy to have a place for the night. *(shakes Simon's hand excitedly, then hurries offstage)*

Simon: *(watches Joseph leave)* I suppose I should have had them register.

Elizabeth: *(walks up to Simon with fabric swatches in her hand)* Simon, didn't you hear me?

(Paige joins them, looking over their shoulders.)

Simon: How could I ever ignore you, my dear? What is it?

Elizabeth: Just look at these samples for the wall treatment Aaron wants to do. There's this, and this one, and — oh, I *really* love this one.

Aaron: Is that the pastel? I think the pastel is to *die* for. I see it on that wall, there, and hanging in the doorway, there. *(gestures toward walls)*

Paige: *(to Simon)* What do you think?

Simon: *(smiles halfheartedly)* I think whatever Elizabeth and Aaron decide will be just fine.

Paige: That's the kind of confidence in our decorators that we like to see. And while Elizabeth and Aaron decide what to do with the walls, let's see what Jacob and Ruth are up to, in the staff quarters of King Herod's palace —

(Paige walks offstage, followed by the others.)

Scene One ends

Scene Two: The Palace

(Scene Two opens on another room in Simon and Elizabeth's quarters at the palace. Ruth and Hildy are conferring, while Jacob is just wandering around the room aimlessly, scratching himself and occasionally picking up a bowl or pot, or other object, which he studies, checking the bottom for a price tag. Hildy is dressed flamboyantly, and wears a shawl over her shoulders.)

Hildy: So what do you think of the floors in here, darling?

Ruth: They're very nice. The stone is so level, and the mosaics here in the center are so pretty —

Jacob: Must have cost a fortune. My tax dollars at work. *(picks up a small object, looks at it, and slips it in a pocket, looking around to make sure no one saw him)*

Hildy: Stone and mosaics are sooo BC, darling. Think modern. How does a floor like this feel on your bare feet in the morning — in the winter?

Ruth: Well, I —

Hildy: Go ahead, take your sandals off. Walk around a little. *(Ruth slips her sandals off and takes a few hesitant steps, while Hildy picks up a clay pot on the table.)* See what I mean? Cold.

Ruth: I guess it *is* a little cold.

(Jacob is wandering around again, not paying attention.)

Hildy: And dangerous. What do you think happens when a floor like this gets wet? *(dumps the clay pot on the floor)*

(Jacob, not looking, steps in the "water," slips, and falls.)

Hildy: See?

85

Ruth: *(doubtfully)* I guess.

(Paige enters the room and goes to Jacob who is lying on the floor.)

Paige: Jacob, dude, this is no time to be lying down on the job. You've got a whole weekend of work to do.

Jacob: I think I broke something. I heard something snap.

Paige: You know what they say in show business — break a leg! *(steps over him, up to Hildy and Ruth)* So, what's the first thing they need to do here, Hildy?

(Jacob struggles to his feet, pulls pieces of the object he'd stolen out of his pocket.)

Jacob: *(to himself)* At least it wasn't my hip.

Hildy: We were just looking at the floors, dear. Oh, so cold and drafty. And slippery. Obviously we can't have this in a bedroom. The bedroom is supposed to be warm and cozy, a sanctuary from the rest of the world. Your own secret hiding place, where you —

Paige: Tick-tock, tick-tock, Hildy. What are you going to do?

Hildy: I have a vision for this room. We can create their own little world, a place different from the whole rest of the palace, where they can retreat and be comfortable.

Paige: And how are you going to do that?

Hildy: From the ground up, dear. I had five tons of dirt delivered to the courtyard this morning, and we — ha, ha, I mean *they* — are going to move all of that dirt into this room and spread it around the floor, about six inches deep.

Jacob: *(stunned)* Five tons of dirt?

Hildy: I know. Breathtaking, isn't it? And once the dirt is in, we're going to plant grass, and some *beautiful* shrubbery over there in the corner. And perhaps there could be a hedge, separating the bed from the sitting area. There's no *end* to the possibilities. It'll be **marvelous.** *(takes off her shawl, sweeps it through the air for emphasis, and throws it on the table)*

Jacob: It'll be nuts. I've spent my whole life working to buy a place that *doesn't* have a dirt floor. Why would they —

Hildy: No room for narrow minds, Jacob — *we're* talking art here. *(to Paige and Ruth)* Let me show you the new furniture I picked out. I came across the most *smashing* lawn furniture in the bazaar in Jerusalem. It's out in the courtyard. *(takes each of them by the arm, starts to lead them away)*

Ruth: *(uncertainly)* I'm not so sure about this —

Hildy: I am. Trust me, darling. *(over her shoulder, to Jacob)* Now be a dear and clean up that water, will you? Somebody could fall and get hurt.

Jacob: *(incredulous, calling to them as they leave)* Somebody already did! Somebody got hurt and wet! *(hearing no reply, he looks around for a moment, picks up her shawl from the table and drops it on the floor, pushes it around with his foot as if he is mopping the floor)* It must be forty degrees in here. Won't Herod spring for a little heat? *(spots a brightly colored robe on one of the chairs, slips it on and wraps it around himself)* That's better. *(starts rummaging around again, turning his back to the audience)*

(The three wise men walk onstage, escorted by two guards. One of the guards points to Jacob.)

Guard 1: That's the Royal Advisor. He's been expecting you.

87

Melchior: Thank you, sir.

Guard 1: Is there anything else, sir?

Melchior: *(hands him a gold coin)* Keep an eye on the camels for us, will you?

Guard 1: *(tests the coin by biting on it, slips it into a pocket)* We'll have them washed and waxed for you, too.

Guard 2: How long do you expect to be here?

Melchior: I really don't know — I don't expect it'll be long. We just need to confer with the advisor.

Guard 2: Well, when you leave, be sure to give the guard your ticket. *(hands him a ticket stub)* The first hour is a flat rate, no matter how long you stay.

(The guards leave. The Magi wait for a moment. then Melchior clears his throat.)

Melchior: A-hem.

Jacob: *(drops whatever he was holding, spins around)* What? I was just looking.

Melchior: A thousand pardons for interrupting you, sir.

Jacob: *(mostly to himself)* Sir?

Melchior: My name is Melchior. This is Gaspar and Balthasar. *(each wise man nods when introduced)* We have arrived from Babylon this very night.

Jacob: Yes?

Gaspar: Surely our messenger reached here to tell you we were coming? I know you must be busy, as King Herod's Royal Advisor, but if you have just a few moments —

Jacob: Royal advisor? Oh, right. *(looks down at his robe, realizes it is far nicer and worth far more than anything he owns)* Yes, I am the Royal Advisor. And the name's Jacob, not Shirley. *(leans forward and peers down the hallway)* I think I can spare a few minutes. What do you need?

Balthasar: Sir, we are from Babylon. Melchior is in the Royal Court, there, Gaspar is head of Philosophy at Tigris U, and I hold the Nebuchednezzar Chair in the Foreign Studies Department at the university. We are here in search of a king.

Jacob: *(points)* Out that door, turn right, and go up the stairs at the end of the hall. Look for the gold-covered doors and the mean-looking guards. Don't forget to knock.

Balthasar: We're not looking for King Herod, sir. We're looking for a much greater king.

Jacob: *(looks over his shoulder)* Greater than King Herod? Look, you don't really want to talk that way in here. Herod's a bit ... moody.

Balthasar: I understand. But truly, we're not here for him. We're looking for a new king, whose birth was proclaimed by the stars.

Gaspar: We saw a sign in the sky — a great star, where there had been none before. Our science tells us that it signifies the birth of a wonderful new king here in Judea, as foretold by prophecy.

Jacob: *(scratches himself absently)* A star, eh? Well, I haven't been out much at night, lately. Does your science give you an address? Judea's a big place.

Gaspar: Your own Hebrew prophets have long foretold the birth of a very special king, in the family line of your King David.

Jacob: The clan of King David began in Bethlehem, but it must be spread to the four corners of the kingdom, and beyond, after all these years. How can you ever hope to find him?

Melchior: By good luck — or divine design — your Emperor Augustus did us the favor of gathering the entire clan in one place at one time. All descendants of that family should be in Bethlehem now, or should be passing through here very soon.

Jacob: Well, good luck finding him. That place is a zoo. Wall to wall people — they're sleeping in the countryside. I can't tell you how many people I've *(pauses)* how many people have been turned away from the inn in Bethlehem.

Melchior: Still, we must look. The star tells us we must find this child.

Jacob: *(thoughtfully)* You're going to need a place to stay while you're in Bethlehem, aren't you?

Gaspar: We will.

Jacob: *(picks up a piece of paper from the table, writes something hastily)* Then let me do you a favor — you know, as Herod's advisor. Take this to the Bethlehem Village Inn, near the main gate. Tell them you have permission to use the innkeeper's own room while you're in town.

Gaspar: *(takes paper)* But won't the innkeeper mind?

Jacob: He won't mind. I know him very well. But just to be fair, why don't you pay him for the room? Nothing too extravagant for men such as yourself — say five shekels a night?

Gaspar: Five shekels? That won't be a problem.

Jacob: Did I say five? I meant ten. Ten shekels a night.

Melchior: I see. Ten it is. And perhaps we'd best leave while it's still ten. *(bows slightly)* Thank you for your ... kindness and generosity, sir. *(looks at the other Magi)* Let's be on our way, we can be there by this afternoon.

(The three wise men leave in a small procession.)

Melchior: *(as they walk out)* Now, does anybody need to use the restroom? I don't want to be stopping every ten minutes.

Gaspar: Hey! It wasn't me last time.

Jacob: *(calls after them)* When you find this new king, let us know. I'm sure King Herod will want to extend his best wishes! *(to himself)* They'll be searching for a month, and I'll get richer every day. *(takes off the robe, drops it on the table)*

(Ruth and Hildy walk back in, with Paige in tow.)

Hildy: *There* you are. Were you planning on joining us?

Jacob: Sure, why not? Things are starting to look up.

Ruth: Well, you seem to be in a better mood.

Jacob: I just decided to go with the flow, Ruth. Just going with the flow.

Paige: And while Jacob and Ruth get ready to go with the flow — and start lugging in five tons of dirt — let's look in on Simon and Elizabeth, and see how they're getting along with Aaron and his plans to revitalize the Bethlehem Village Inn's common room.

Scene Two ends

91

Scene Three: The Inn

(Scene Three opens with Elizabeth sitting at a table in the foreground, sewing, with Aaron in the background measuring windows in the walls. Simon is not visible. Paige approaches Elizabeth.)

Paige: So here we are, late in Day One, and it looks like they've put you to work, Elizabeth. How is it going?

Elizabeth: We're not as far as I'd hoped we'd be, but I guess it's Okay. I've got another three window treatments to do and then a tablecloth and some placemats. But I don't know if we're going to make it.

Aaron: *(approaches them)* Don't you believe her, Paige, she's doing a *fabulous* job. *(leans over and hugs Elizabeth briefly)* She's a real trooper. I wish we had five more like her.

Paige: And where's Simon? I don't see him.

Aaron: Oh, him. He's reweaving the chair seats, out back. I just *had* to get him out of here. There's just way too much negative energy flowing out of that man. He is like a bad karma magnet.

Simon: *(from offstage)* Aaron! Aaron! Come here, there's something wrong. These seats don't look right.

Aaron: And did I mention he's completely worthless? He probably wove his fingers into one of the seats. I —

Simon: *(offstage)* Aaron, I really need help!

Aaron: *(loudly)* Coming! *(to Paige)* I'm sorry, I have to go see what he's gotten into. *(exits)*

Elizabeth: *(reluctantly)* I'm afraid there have been some personality conflicts.

Paige: So I see. I hope they don't keep you from finishing your room.

Elizabeth: Oh, they won't. Don't worry about that. We'll stay up all night if we have to.

Paige: I'm afraid it may come to that — and I know Aaron will make sure you finish. Now I'd better see what's happening out back. *(exits)*

(The three Magi approach Elizabeth from the other direction.)

Melchior: Is this the Bethlehem Village Inn?

Elizabeth: Yes it is. Can I help you?

Melchior: I have this note — my friends and I have permission to spend the night in the innkeeper's room. If you could just show us where it is?

Elizabeth: *(looks at note)* Well — this seems a little strange. But Jacob said you could use it?

Gaspar: Yes, he did. We're going to be in Bethlehem for a while, and we didn't have a place to stay. He was nice enough to arrange for us to get this room.

Elizabeth: Well — I guess it will be okay, if he says so. The innkeeper's room is back there, to the left.

Balthasar: Thank you, ma'am. *(hands her a bag of coins)* And here is a week's rent, as he suggested.

Elizabeth: *(opens bag, looks surprised)* Okay, now this is making more sense. You look tired — go on and get some rest. I'll have someone take your beasts down to the stable.

Melchior: Are you sure, ma'am? Truth is, we are very tired. It's been a long trip, and we spent most of this afternoon searching through Bethlehem and the countryside around it.

Elizabeth: And did you find what you were looking for?

Gaspar: Not yet, but we will. The stars don't lie, and neither do the great prophecies.

Elizabeth: *(begins sewing again)* I'm sure you will. There's bread and fruit in the kitchen and fresh water on the table.

Balthasar: Thank you, ma'am. *(bows)* We appreciate your hospitality.

(There is no answer, so the three wise men depart in the direction Elizabeth pointed. A few moments later Simon enters from a different direction.)

Simon: Did I hear voices?

Elizabeth: Yes, just some more travelers. These three had a note from Jacob, allowing them to stay in his room. And a week's rent.

Simon: I'm not surprised. He would rent out his mother's room, for the right price. Are they here for the census?

Elizabeth: I don't think so. They said they're looking for someone, or something.

Simon: Good luck finding them around here. This village seems to get fuller by the hour.

Elizabeth: I'm sure it'll work out for them.

Simon: Anyway, it's not our problem. Can you come out? Aaron wants to give us our homework for the night.

94

Elizabeth: Sure, just a second. *(stands up and starts to walk after Simon; the curtain follows her, sewn to her clothes)*

Simon: *(turns to look at her)* Nice look.

Elizabeth: Don't push your luck. It's going to be a long night, and there's no guarantee you have to live through it. *(rips the curtain off her clothing; they both exit)*

Scene Three ends

Scene Four: The Inn

(Scene Four opens at the Inn. Simon is seated in a chair, leaning back, with his head back, mouth open, and snoring softly; there is fabric in his lap. Aaron is seated with his head on the table, cushioned by his arms. Jacob and Ruth sneak in. Jacob is in one of Simon's robes; there is dirt on his face.)

Jacob: *(after a shh motion)* See, I told you they'd be asleep.

Ruth: I still don't feel right about this.

Jacob: I told you, one quick look and we're out of here. After I saw what we were doing to *their* place, I just *had* to see what they were doing here.

Ruth: It doesn't look too bad. Let's go. *(tries to leave)*

Jacob: Sure. Just let me check the till and make sure they put the money from those Babylonians in there. *(starts to sneak past Simon)*

Simon: *(wakes with a start)* I'm awake! I'm awake! I was just resting my eyes. *(looks around)* What? Who? You aren't supposed to be here!

Jacob: Shhh. We just wanted to see how the room was coming.

Simon: Isn't that against the rules?

Ruth: That's what I tried to tell him.

Jacob: It's my home. I should be able to see what you're doing to it.

Simon: So far, lots of window and wall treatments. That man is obsessed with fabrics. *(holds up a hand)* I can't tell you how many times I've stuck myself with these darn needles.

Ruth: Okay, then, let's go. I don't want to get caught.

Jacob: Hildy won't be waking up for a while. I put enough sleeping powder in her water to put down an elephant.

Simon: Since you're here, how is our bedroom coming along?

Jacob: That depends. Do you think of yourself as an outdoorsy person?

(Simon looks puzzled, but before he can answer Joseph rushes into the room.)

Joseph: Please! I need some help, here.

Jacob: You? I thought I turned you away a couple of days ago.

Joseph: You did. But *he (points to Simon)* told us we could stay. My wife and I are in the stable.

Jacob: *(admiringly)* The stable, eh? I never thought of renting that out. How much did you get for it?

96

Simon: Nothing. They seemed like a nice couple, and they needed a place to stay. His wife is pregnant.

Joseph: And I think she's going to have the baby now! We need help.

Jacob: Nothing? Do you know how big that stable is? I could have fit three or four families in there.

Elizabeth: We're going to need some clean cloths.

Simon: Well, I know someone who's got plenty of nice, new cloth. Aaron! Aaron! Wake up!

Aaron: *(raises his head groggily)* I didn't do it. And if I did, I didn't mean to. What?

Simon: We have a woman giving birth. Do you have some fabric we can use?

Aaron: What, are you going to make him a little sailor suit? Trust me, it'll take *you* forever to sew anything. Honestly, if this man were any clumsier he wouldn't be able to feed himself. He's about as coordinated as a pig wearing mittens.

Simon: Focus, here. We don't need the fabric to make clothes.

Ruth: We need something to wrap around him, once the baby is born. Something soft and warm.

Aaron: I have some white linen. *(sorts through the fabric on the table, comes up with white material)* This was going to be used as an accent on the chair covers. It was going to look *fabulous*.

Ruth: It'll look even better around a baby. Come with me. Jacob, you stay with the men. *(Ruth and Aaron hurry away)*

Joseph: *(nervously)* Is there something I should be doing? I feel like I should be doing something.

Jacob: Is this your first?

Joseph: Yes, and it was kind of a surprise, all things considered.

Simon: What do you mean?

Joseph: It's a long story. Should I be doing something to help?

Jacob: The kitchen is back that way. We're going to need boiling water — lots of it.

Joseph: Right. Boiling water. I can do that. *(hurries out)*

Simon: So you have children?

Jacob: Four. We've been through this a few times. My wife is very good — she'll be able to help keep things under control.

Simon: So what's the boiling water for?

Jacob: *(smiles)* By the time he brings in wood, stokes the fire, draws water, and gets it to boil, it should all be over. And then all he has to do is go down and admire his child. He'll never even ask what the water was for.

Simon: Oh. You know, I've always wondered about that.

Elizabeth: *(walks onstage; sleepily)* What's all the excitement? I heard someone in the kitchen. Jacob? What are you doing here?

Simon: It's a long story, dear. But that young couple from Nazareth is having their baby tonight.

Elizabeth: Oh my. It's a good thing we made a place for them to stay, then. Is there anything I can do to help?

Simon: You could go down to the stable to see. I'm sure they could use an extra pair of hands.

Elizabeth: I will. Thanks. *(exits)*

Jacob: She seems excited. Do you have children?

Simon: No. My job made it difficult — I thought it was so important that I couldn't make time for kids. Like this weekend. I was sure that I couldn't be away from the palace this long, but everything seems to be going along fine.

Jacob: You haven't seen your bedroom yet.

Simon: What?

Jacob: Never mind. You were saying?

Simon: Just that I'm not irreplaceable. For instance, there was this delegation coming from Babylon that I was supposed to meet with. A group of scholars, looking for some new prophet, or something.

Jacob: Oh?

Simon: Yes. Herod wanted me to meet with them and pump them for information — without helping them. But even without me there, things must have worked out anyway. I'll have to find out what happened.

Jacob: So, when you say you weren't supposed to help them — what does that mean?

Simon: Why?

Jacob: Well, I think I may have talked to them. And I — uh — may have found them a place to stay, while they look for this new king of theirs.

Simon: New king? That's what Herod was afraid of. What did they tell you?

Jacob: That they were looking for a new king that had just been born, or was about to be born. They were following a sign in the sky, and some old Hebrew prophecies.

Simon: That would be the Messiah, then. The great leader, the savior of our people. That's not what King Herod wanted to hear. Where were they going to be staying?

(Jacob hesitates, then points down the hall.)

Simon: They're the travelers in your room!

Jacob: *(apologetically)* I'm afraid so.

Simon: Oh-oh. Now I'm going to have to figure out what to do about that. King Herod has certain expectations, as I'm sure you can imagine.

Jacob: Sorry if I made any trouble.

Simon: It may not be a problem, if we can just send them on their way. Whatever we do, we can't let them find this king — if they're right.

Jacob: They seemed pretty sure of themselves.

Simon: All the more reason to worry.

(Elizabeth hurries in.)

Elizabeth: Where's Joseph?

Simon: In the kitchen. Why?

Elizabeth: Because he's a new father, and he needs to see his son. And you need to see, too.

Simon: I've seen babies before.

Elizabeth: Not like this.

(Elizabeth goes back toward the kitchen. Simon and Jacob look at one another for a moment, then leave for the stable.)

Scene Four ends

Scene Five: The Stable
(Scene Five opens at the stable, where Aaron is standing outside, dabbing at his forehead. Shepherds are standing there, as well. Mary is propped up in the back, cradling a baby in her arms, with Ruth kneeling next to her.)

Simon: What's all this?

Aaron: It's a nightmare. I never saw anything like it. And my material — it's *ruined*!

Simon: Why don't you go back up the inn and get something to drink?

Aaron: And then I'm going to need a nap. This was *exhausting*. *(exits)*

Jacob: *(to Shepherd 1)* Who are you and what are you doing here?

101

Shepherd 1: We are shepherds from the hills west of Bethlehem, sir. We came here because we were sent.

Jacob: Sent by who?

Shepherd 2: We were tending our flocks and all of a sudden there was this blinding white light in the heavens.

Jacob: The star?

Simon: Star?

Jacob: The sign in the heavens that the Babylonians were following.

Shepherd 3: Not the star, sir. We've seen it, ourselves, in the last couple of weeks, but it was much brighter than that.

Shepherd 4: This light was brighter than the sun at midday, and it lit up the meadow around us, so bright that it hurt our eyes.

Jacob: What was it?

Shepherd 1: I've never seen anything like it — but it was the glory of God.

Simon: The glory of God?

Shepherd 2: Yes. God was there. And all of a sudden I could see a shape like a man in the sky, and this voice came out of the light. It was like thunder — so loud I almost had to cover my ears — but I couldn't move. I just stood there and listened — too scared to move.

Shepherd 3: And then the voice said: "Don't be afraid. I bring you glad tidings of great joy. The Savior, the Messiah, is born tonight in Bethlehem, the city of David."

Simon: The Messiah?

Shepherd 4: Yes. And then the voice said, "This is how you will recognize him — you will find a baby lying in a manger, wrapped in swaddling cloths."

Shepherd 1: And then suddenly there were more of them — more angels than we could count, singing, "Glory to God in the highest heaven, and on earth peace and good will toward mankind."

(As they're speaking, Joseph and Elizabeth come onto the scene. Joseph hurries in to be with Mary; Elizabeth stays out with Simon.)

Shepherd 2: And so we come to worship this new wonder — this Messiah who will grow up to save all humankind — King of all kings.

Simon: King of kings? Hmm *(He hesitates, then leans over and whispers something to Elizabeth. She looks uncertain, and then leaves quickly.)*

Shepherd 3: We followed the light in the heavens, until we came to this place. And there, just as we had been told, there was a child in the manger.

Ruth: *(comes out)* When they told me what had happened, I knew this was no ordinary child. So I sent Elizabeth for all of you.

Jacob: It sounds like the new king that the Babylonians were looking for, doesn't it?

Simon: Yes, it does. And it sounds like the new king Herod was afraid of, too.

Paige: *(comes onstage)* So *there* you are! We've been looking all over for you. You're supposed to be working on your rooms, not ... not ... whatever you're doing here. What *are* you doing here?

Jacob: Something a little more important seems to have come up, Paige. I'm sorry.

Paige: I'm sorry, too, but you have some obligations here. You're supposed to be working on your rooms.

Jacob: I just don't think those obligations are very important, tonight. Sorry.

Paige: *(horrified)* Not important? But this is TV! There isn't anything more important than that. This is *reality* TV.

Jacob: No it's not. Dumping five tons of dirt into a man's bedroom isn't reality.

Simon: Wha —?

Jacob: Never mind. Swapping rooms so some half-crazy designers can indulge their whims isn't reality. *That's* reality in there. *(points toward Mary and the baby)* That's a new life coming into the world. Maybe even new life coming for the whole world.

Paige: *(stares at him)* Mister, I don't know what your problem is, but you've got some seriously warped views of the world. We're done here. *(walks away in disgust)*

(The Magi walk past her, with Elizabeth.)

Melchior: *(to Simon)* Your wife said we were to come to the stable at once.

Simon: Jacob tells me you're looking for some kind of newborn king.

Melchior: That's right. Your Hebrew prophets called him the Messiah, the Savior.

Gaspar: He will be born in the town of Bethlehem, in the line of King David.

Balthasar: He will be a great king that will rule over all the earth, and bring God's kingdom to earth.

Simon: I see. I think your man is in there. The little one, wrapped in swaddling clothes.

(The Magi seem startled for a moment, then approach Mary and the baby. They kneel, still at a distance.)

Melchior: What is the name of this child?

Mary: We will call him Jesus.

Melchior: *(bows down)* We are blessed.

(The lights go down, and Simon and Jacob walk away from the stable.)

Jacob: I'd say they found what they were looking for.

Simon: I'd say they've found a lot more than we really know. I have a funny feeling we're going to be hearing more from that little guy in there — some day.

Jacob: What are you going to tell King Herod?

Simon: Nothing much to tell, is there? I wasn't at the palace this weekend, I was busy sewing window treatments. And I've got the wounds to prove it. By the time he knows anything about this, they'll be long gone. *(pauses)* Funny, isn't it?

Jacob: What?

PSIA information can be obtained at www.ICGtesting.com
Printed in the USA
VOW07s1451030913

50793LV00009B/100/P

9 780788 024832

Simon: A day ago, we were ready to spend hundreds of shekels and days of our time to try to change our worlds. And this little baby comes along and does it all by himself, in just a moment of time — just by coming into the world.

Jacob: *(smiles)* Now that's the kind of reality I can deal with.

(The two men clasp hands and walk back into the stable.)

The End